CONTENTS

INTRODUCTION

If you, like me, have ever felt that sense of panic when your kids stare up at you and ask 'what are we going to do now?', then this is the book for you. Hi. I'm Claire, Mum to two girls and I am the sort of person who likes to have a plan for everything. As a teacher, I am always trying out new ways to make learning engaging and fun. Some work, and some don't, and it is this valuable process of trial and error that has developed my practice and also my ability to cope in the classroom.

Before I had kids, I didn't think it would be too hard to think ahead and source great ideas for how to spend our time together. And then I had kids. Very quickly, I realized that having an idea was one thing and carrying it out was quite another. I hadn't foreseen the moments when my kids would turn their little noses up at a plan I had concocted or when the activity I had intended to last until lunchtime took ten minutes and was over by 9am.

I know I am not alone. Parents all around the world are constantly being asked 'what now?' by their kids, who in turn look to their grown-ups and expect a reply. It is a question that seems so simple to ask and yet can be so incredibly hard to answer. And it is also a question that is not going anywhere fast. Parenting is a round the clock job, and our kids will rely on us for solutions until they are old enough to answer it for themselves.

And the struggle really is real. With kids, weekends that used to be full of rest and relaxation become punctuated with a constant demand for things to do, and school holidays easily morph into an endless empty calendar that needs filling. The relentlessness of needing great ideas, and fast, is for me, one of the most challenging aspects of parenthood and it is the main reason this book exists.

In March 2020, when lockdown was on the horizon, I began to worry about how I would find answers to the inevitable 'what now' question if we were stuck at home for days on end. My solution was to set up a Facebook group, which I called Family Lockdown Tips & Ideas, to share suggestions and strategies to cope. I never expected that within a month, the group would have over a million members from around the world, sharing some of the most innovative and inspirational ideas I have ever seen. I could also not have anticipated the astonishing level of support members, who have never met, have shown each other, which has made the community an incredibly welcoming place to be. From DIY board games, to playgrounds made of pallets, to creating holidays at home, the group showcased what is possible, despite the challenging circumstances.

What became clear is that you don't need to go out and spend money to have fun, nor do you need elaborate equipment and a detailed itinerary to enjoy family time together. Sometimes the only resources you need are the items around you, the things you already have which are so easy to overlook. I am the sort of parent who was always on the hunt for the next new thing to entertain my kids. And now I look around me and see my box of recycling as a treasure trove for crafts, my freezer as a storage cabinet for ice play and the nature in my garden as an endless free resource for everyday art. This seismic shift in my outlook has been the key to unlocking ideas for what to do next, and has revolutionized the way I parent and spend time with my own family, for the better.

There is no 'one size fits all' way to fill your time with your kids. All families are totally unique and the sort of thing that might float your boat on the first Monday morning of the school holidays might sink someone else's. However what we all have in common is the need for answers and solutions to the universal question of what to do next. And this book, I hope, will provide you with just that. My family has had great fun experimenting with and testing out the ideas and I hope you find them really enjoyable, super useful and that ultimately they help you to make time at home with your family the best it can possibly be.

Claire x

HOW TO USE THIS BOOK

The aim of this book is to equip you with great ideas for what you can do at home as a family to enjoy your time together and arm you with the confidence and best strategies to make them work. There is no pressure, judgement or expectation, as every child has a long list of likes and dislikes, as do their parents! And, we all know, even with the best of intentions, things don't always quite work out how we'd like or planned for.

Saying that, kids are highly adaptable, malleable and naturally curious. They constantly surprise us, challenge us and, if mine are anything to go by, encourage us to see the world through their fresh eyes. Despite the fact that kids often love to be in charge and get what they want, deep down they crave guidance, reassurance and answers – don't we all! And that is where I hope this book can step in and be useful. To give you the confidence you need to show them what to do, how to do it and feel as calm and capable about the results as any parent can be.

Over the course of a day, we engage in many different activities at different times for different reasons. And the same is true of our kids. Sometimes, we crave something quiet and introspective to get on with, whereas at other times all we want to do is move our bodies and, in the words of my five-year-old, 'shake the sillies out'. Sometimes a breath of fresh air and an earthy nature activity outside will be just what they need whereas at other times, something quieter involving paper, paint and pens will suit them best. This book reflects that variety.

Each chapter embraces a different type of activity you can do at home and the aim of that is not just so that there is a little something for everyone (although I hope that is true too), but so that the variety of what goes into a family day at home is represented, with a good plan to go with it.

At the very heart of this book is the desire to see family time at home as something to embrace with open arms. I've spent years fearing rainy weekends, long summer holidays and, in general, just those gaps of time in between everything else that don't have a micro-plan of their own. And I've come to see that this panic is pointless. It doesn't lead to greatness and it certainly doesn't benefit my kids. Having a few really good ideas up my sleeve and the confidence to do them has meant that I can look forward to family time at home. The activities in this book reflect this. They are there to remind you that you can totally do it, and that process of doing something together is as important, if not more, than the result.

I haven't labelled any activities with the ages they are suitable for and there is a very good reason for this. I suppose, on the one hand, I am no expert in childhood development and I don't know the academic reasons behind why an art activity would be better suited for a three-year-old than a six-year-old. However, I am a (secondary school) teacher, and what I find works well for me in the classroom are activities that can be stretched to suit the needs of each child. It is a practice I adopt at home with my own kids. My two-year-old often does the same activity as her five-year-old sister, just needing more guidance, care and support.

This thinking underpins the ideas in this book. Kids develop in different ways at different times and have things that they find more difficult to do than others. I always enjoyed art as a child however was quite happy to sit out of any sporting activity, and I have friends who were the exact opposite. The message, therefore, is to give things a go. Experiment and see what your kids can and like to do. Even just by watching you do something, they are learning and developing and so you can set them a brilliant example, just by trying out something new.

I probably shouldn't admit this but I do have a favourite chapter. That's not to say for a second the others aren't good. They are. I think. Please read and enjoy the activities and ideas in all of them. But the chapter called 'The Great Indoors' is the closest to my heart. During the coronavirus pandemic lockdown, families all over the world embraced the challenges of being at home by re-creating trips and adventures without leaving their front door. The results were incredible. And so this chapter is both inspired by and dedicated to them and best represents the way in which we can, together, re-brand family time at home as a thing of joy. Or at least until our kids start whining and asking if it's time for dinner yet.

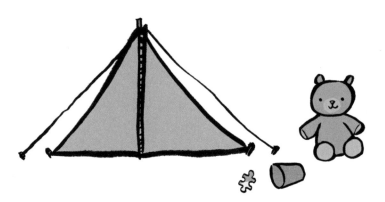

And so without further ado, I'd love you flick through the colourful pages and have fun considering what you might do next. We've honestly had so much fun trying them all out and as someone who is not a natural when it comes to crafts, setting up a science experiment or thinking up imaginative physical activities, I've learnt so much about the importance of just giving things a go. Some of the activities, such as salt painting, nature picture frames and afternoon tea, are some of our 'go to' weekend activities whereas making dandelion honey or camping are the sort of activities I would plan ahead for slightly. There are lots of simple ideas in here to pep up a playdate and the most important ingredient to make all of them work, is the willingness to give something new a try.

And so let that be your guide. Just by getting this far, you have embraced what is possible and I am genuinely excited for what you might do. And if you want to tell me, I'd love for you to share it on the Facebook group. This will help continue the cycle of inspiration, so that parents around the world can act as a team, to answer that question that we all face, 'what are we going to do now?' And this time, have some answers.

USEFUL
RESOURCES
TO HAVE

A bit like having a list of ingredients for a recipe to make a cake, having a range of resources at home can make life so much easier when you're faced with kids asking you what to do. I have spent a lot of time working out what resources are the best value, most versatile and useful for family fun so you don't have to. I've tried to keep this book as simple as possible when it comes to the resources needed, as having kids is expensive enough, plus when an activity doesn't quite go according to plan, it can be incredibly disheartening if a lot of effort has gone into making it happen.

Whilst we're on the topic of buying resources, I would always say where possible use what you have. Save cardboard boxes from your recycling and stack them up out of the way, keep a plastic bag of loo rolls somewhere dry, save up bottle tops, wrapping paper and small yoghurt pots and keep old magazines as they are great for crafting and collaging.

Here is a list of a few of my essentials. These are the things that if you have, you have a plan. They are all used at one point or another in this book and they are common items that are not hard to find.

ARTS AND CRAFTS

- **WASHABLE POSTER PAINTS:** I know you can buy nice little neat bottles for small hands, but I don't find them very cost effective. I buy big bottles and decant when I need to use them. I'm much less precious about how much we use this way and encourage my girls to experiment more when I am confident that we won't run out. Hand soap dispensers are a brilliant way to pump paint when you need it and keep it stored between art sessions, or you could use old ketchup bottles too.

- **PAINTBRUSHES AND SPONGES:** It is good to have a variety of paintbrushes, which can be bought incredibly cheaply and are widely available. I tend to buy two sets of everything when I shop, one for now and one for just in case or when it breaks. This is true of paintbrushes. I can't handle the squabbling over my kids wanting the same brush at the same time!

- **A PLASTIC SHOWER CURTAIN:** These make great surfaces to paint on as they are largely waterproof, easy to clean, cover a big surface and are very inexpensive. I got a large apple-green shower curtain in the sale for 99p and I still use it every time we plan a task that could be messy.

- **PLAIN AND COLOURED PAPER:** We have a stack of plain paper which is accessible to our kids anytime they want to draw and then we keep the coloured paper on a surface much higher up as I like to use it sparingly.

- **PVA GLUE:** This type of glue is so versatile as it not only sticks things together but it can be used to give things a nice sheen when it is dry. It can be mixed up with paint to form a coloured glue and you can use a spatula. However I tend to use paintbrushes to apply PVA glue, and wash them quickly afterwards before they dry.

- **A GLUE GUN:** You don't need to be a serious crafter to have a glue gun. Far from it. I use my glue gun all the time, from fixing broken toys to sticking the handle back on my favourite mug. They are a small investment but the sort of thing you'll question how you lived without beforehand.

- **LOLLY STICKS:** These can, in addition to being used for fruit kebabs and being stuck in small yoghurts to make ice lollies, be incredibly useful for lots of different games and look great stuck on paper too.

- **STICKERS:** We buy cheap stickers in bulk as both my kids love them and will literally spend hours playing and making art with them. They are an easy go-to decoration and can spruce up home-made gifts very well.

- **PACK OF BLANK CARDS AND ENVELOPES:** We usually make our own greeting cards which is a great thing to do, as you never have to remember to buy them for birthdays and whatnot. They come in different colours and sizes, however we tend to buy A6-sized white ones.

- **FELT-TIP PENS:** I don't have any specific recommendations for pens other than not to buy any that have tricky lids to put back on. I have a house strewn with un-lidded pens and so I'm always on the hunt for new ones.

- **PIPE CLEANERS:** One afternoon when I had run out of things to do and was feeling exasperated, I chucked a pile of pipe cleaners on the kitchen table and told my kids to 'go for it'. And they did, making bracelets, crowns and flowers. Pipe cleaners are great 'fixers' to tie things together when you don't want glue and are simple to snip to size.

KITCHEN CUPBOARD

- **PLAIN PAPER PLATES:** The humble paper plate has so many uses, from masks to dreamcatchers to a paint palette, they are so handy to have around. We buy them in bulk and I find them easy to pop into a bag with some pencils or pens for a contained art activity out and about.

- **BIODEGRADABLE STRAWS:** These are super handy, not just for the activities in this book, but to use for drinking as well as blowing through to make bubbles or sticking down on paper plates in a pattern to make a marble run.

- **FOOD COLOURING:** I recently bought a set of twelve pots of food colouring and I haven't looked back. We've used them for everything, from dying shaving foam for marbling (check the Achievable Art chapter) to sprucing up bath time by turning the water a bright shade of teal (don't worry, a few drops won't stain!). When you've got a great set of colours, you'll find all sorts of uses for them you didn't know possible.

- **CORNFLOUR:** There are lots of craft recipes that use cornflour, such as chalk paint, Oobleck (see Whizzy Science for more details), play dough and so on. It is more than just versatile. It is a store-cupboard staple.

- **SELF-RAISING AND PLAIN FLOUR:** They are the basis to so many recipes (some of which are included in this book) and craft activities such as making clay and salt dough. Even just by adding water to make a smooth dough, you can make flatbreads on a frying pan. Plus, did I mention cake!

- **ZIP-LOCK BAGS:** A good zip-lock bag can help you organize your life. That really isn't an understatement. From bagging up toiletries, toys, pieces and puzzles, to acting as a pencil case, they really are so handy.

- **ICE-CUBE TRAYS:** The traditional solid ice-cube tray can make a great paint palette and is used quite a bit in this book for freezing things, from toys to coloured ice for ice painting. I've been known to serve up snacks in mine!

STORAGE

Having the right storage for resources for activities does make doing them a whole lot easier. Don't overthink it. Your storage doesn't need to be Instagrammable or Pinterest worthy. It just needs to work for you and your kids. For craft, we have an IKEA Kallax unit with see-through plastic tubs, which are labelled, so that we know what is inside. I do tend to buy pots, jars and storage boxes whenever I see one that I like and can afford and save the ones that look handy from the recycling (an egg box is great for small craft items like sequins and pom-poms!). And so allow yourself to look around your home, and think about how best you could use your space to make it more likely that activities will be easy to do. The easier it is to access what you need, the more likely you are to give it a go. Or at least that is what happens in my experience.

MEASURING

Trying to measure out ingredients with your kids hanging off you can feel like trying to walk a tightrope in the middle of a storm. I know it is good for kids to help you with measuring out ingredients, in a 'maths on the go' sort of way, however where possible, I like to opt for the American-style system of using cups. Yes, they are less precise but, boy, are they simple to use.

In this book, quite a few of the activities require using a ratio of ingredients, for example, two cups of X to one cup of Y. Whenever that is the case, it doesn't matter whether you use a mug, cup, tumbler or small bowl. So long as the ratios are accurate, the mixture should work. The recipe for lemonade scones in The Great Indoors chapter, for example, uses mugs for flour, cream and lemonade, although any cup will do, so long as you use the same one each time.

DOCUMENTING FAMILY TIME

I have, literally, tens of thousands of unsorted photos on my phone, and very few of these feature me with my kids, and even fewer with my husband present too. And yet my kids are obsessed with looking at photos from when they were little and, as a history teacher, I know how important documents are in telling the story of the past. So consider this a plea, from me to you, to tell you to take as many photos of you and your family together, doing these activities or doing nothing at all. Every moment you capture will help you to remember your time together and the fun you had. And I'm sure you don't need me to tell you just how fast kids grow up.

USEFUL ICONS

I have added some icons to the top of each page to help give a quick reference as you flick through, as to what you can expect from each activity.

TRASH INTO TREASURE
Give pre-loved stuff a new lease of life by reusing and recycling

WOW FACTOR
Guaranteed to enthral and intrigue, these activities have that little something extra

FAST & FUN
Go-to activities that you can set up in minutes

MESSY
A warning! These may be a little messier than the rest, but I assure you they are worth it

CALMING
Great for quiet afternoons

BLOW OUT THE COBWEBS
For when everyone has lots of energy and nowhere to put it

PLAN AHEAD
A little forward planning goes a long way

INVOLVES FOOD
Not only are these fun to do, they also result in edible treats

HOURS OF FUN
Fun to make in the first place and then can be played with again and again

FIND THE JIGSAW PIECES

There are 25 jigsaw pieces hidden throughout, see how many you can find.

WHAT CHAPTER AM I IN?

Along with headings and colour-coding, there is a fox at the corner of every page. He has different accessories to help you navigate quickly through the different chapters. Wellbeing Wonders is a personal favourite.

ACHIEVABLE ART

You don't need to be arty to do art with your kids. Trust me, I'm not. But I do love to doodle and draw (often when I should be listening) and I find something about being creative both freeing and therapeutic. I don't have a neatly organized craft cupboard brimming with supplies or a beautifully curated mosaic of my kids' pictures framed on the wall (they're haphazardly stuck to the fridge, in case you were wondering). But I do have an enthusiasm for my kids doing art whenever they can. Saying that, there is no escaping the fact that art with kids can be incredibly stressful: pots of water tipping over, marker pens on the walls and paint splodges on the cat. With this in mind, all the ideas here have been tried and tested to give you great results with minimal faff. They do not require any specific skills or hard-to-get resources. And having done them all with my own kids, I'm certain there is no lower or upper age limit, although being able to hold a paintbrush does help. I really hope you enjoy them and can relax into the process of creating and building memories together, whatever the outcome.

MASKING TAPE MAGIC

I never thought I'd say this but I think I have a masking tape problem. I use it for so many things, from making hopscotch in my hallway to racetracks on my living room floor, and of course for DIY projects too. I even have a favourite brand, FrogTape, which gives super clean lines and has saved my unsteady hand on many an occasion. Here, using masking tape on canvas or card, and letting your kids do what they want on top of it, is a stress-free way of letting them have fun and giving you something for your wall that will look a lot more skilful than you might expect!

WHAT YOU NEED

- Masking tape
- Paints – traditional poster paint is great for this
- Paintbrushes or sponges
- Surface to paint on – canvas, card or lining paper

HOW IT WORKS

1. The trick here is to lay your masking tape down on your surface in a pattern of your choice before anything else happens. Masking tape can be quite adhesive and can damage paper quite easily, and so my top tip is to stick your masking tape to a piece of clothing first, to reduce the adhesion, and avoid your paper ripping later.

2. Now you can choose your masking tape shapes. You could opt for lots of crisscrossed lines, you could spell out a letter or date, you could go for stripes for fun, or maybe to represent trees in a forest. Whatever appeals most to you and your kids.

3. Now this is the really fun bit. Your kids paint onto the surface in whichever way they choose, right over the masking tape, which you will peel back at the end. If the masking tape pattern makes distinct sections on the surface, they could paint each section in a different colour. They could flick paint at the surface in the style of Jackson Pollock. They could paint something more figurative like a sunset or tree, although remind them that the masking tape will be removed and to expect that. Little kids can smear paint over the surface using sponges or bigger paintbrushes.

4. The big reveal! Slowly pull the masking tape back at a 90-degree angle to the paper. It is better to do this when the paint is fully dry. If it is still wet, you can end up peeling back blobs of paint with the tape.

5. Depending on your piece, you can add decorations with felt-tip pens by drawing outlines where the tape was, or adding stickers, glitter or tissue paper. My preference would be to keep it simple and enjoy the colour against neat clean lines.

SHORT OF TIME

You can reveal some beautiful art by cutting out shapes, letters or numbers from a piece of paper painted in an abstract style. Let your kids experiment with mixing paints on paper, swirling, blending and combining a few different colours before leaving it to dry. The freedom of abstract painting is great for kids of all ages as there is no right or wrong way to do it and they don't need to worry about being neat or staying within the lines. When the paint is dry, you can cut out shapes, letters or numbers to play with, use as decoration or just stick down on fresh paper to create a scene or something memorable. This looks really effective on black paper, as the coloured shapes contrast sharply against the dark background.

MELTED CRAYON MASTERPIECE

I have a confession. I really don't like crayons. They snap between little fingers, they smash when dropped, they've ruined the inside of practically every bag I own and go blunt in seconds. We're definitely a 'felt-tip family' at this end (although don't get me started on finding the lids). You can get your own back on these waxy little fiends by melting the tips and creating some seriously lovely art, without any messy hands. In short, you glue crayons down to a surface and apply heat to the tips so that they will slowly melt and drip down to create a rainbow rain effect. These simple steps will help you make an art installation for your wall, without a scribble in sight.

WHAT YOU NEED

• Crayons: Two crayons take up around 1cm when placed side by side. So measure your surface in centimetres and double the number to see how many crayons you'll need in total. It is also helpful to have spare crayons to hand and to practise on! Note: Different brands have different melting points. It is worth doing a quick trial beforehand.

• Surface of your choice: You need a robust surface to stick your crayons on. It could be a canvas, a piece of MDF or wood, or some thick card. The back of a delivery box would work well. Paint it white or a very light colour, to show up the colours of the crayons better.

- Hairdryer, ideally one where you can control the heat.
- Glue: You can stick your crayons down using any strong glue, such as Gorilla glue, however a craft glue gun is ideal.
- An old shower curtain or plenty of newspaper to cover the floor, as the crayons may splatter.

HOW IT WORKS

1. Practice: Get your kids to help you to line up your crayons on a flat surface in the colour order you like best. Make sure the tips are pointing downwards, as this is the direction that they will drip. I've done this with the traditional rainbow colours in a line and also in a heart shape where the flat side of the crayon faces inwards with the tips sticking outwards.

2. Put a line of glue on the back of each crayon and stick it in place on the surface. If your kids are old enough to use a glue gun, they could help you with this. Otherwise, this is a task for the grown-ups. If you want the crayon labels to match each other, make sure you pop the glue in the same place on each crayon. Leave your crayons to dry. They should feel pretty secure before you attempt any melting.

3. Now is the time to decide if you want anything else on your surface. A silhouette of an umbrella, with or without a person holding it, is a popular choice. A house, some trees or even a simple heart also work well. You can draw this on and colour it with black marker or paint, or cut out your chosen shape and stick it on.

4. If you do opt for a silhouette, you might want to protect it from getting splattered with melted crayons and so covering it with some card and masking tape is a good idea. You then remove this at the end.

5. Ask your kids to cover the space you are working in with the shower curtain or newspaper, as the crayons do tend to splatter a bit. Prop up the surface so that it is vertical to the floor because you want the colours running straight down. If you've chosen a shape, you might need to turn your surface around as you go.

6. Now it is time to 'hair-dry' those crayons! This might take a little while but it will definitely be worth it. My advice is to go for it on the hottest setting and point the nozzle at the tips of the crayons. You'll probably find that some colours melt more quickly than others, and if there are any blobs, you can smooth them out with the hairdryer as you go. Involve your kids as much or as little as you'd like at this stage. Older kids might be able to hold the hairdryer, whereas younger kids might like to be the 'crayon-melting monitor', and tell you what they see.

7. When you're happy with your melted crayons, leave them to cool and harden fully before removing any silhouette you've used. Now the tough decision will be where to hang your new colourful family masterpiece!

SHORT OF TIME

If you've got a silicone ice-cube tray (any shape or size) or silicone cupcake cases, this is a super simple way to make new crayons out of old ones! Remove any wrappers from the crayons and then break them up into smallish pieces – around 1–2cm – and place in the tray or cases. Pop in the oven at 200°C and watch them melt, which should take around 10 minutes. Take them out of the tray or cases when totally cool and hard to the touch. Your kids will be the proud owners of multi-coloured reimagined crayons, which they can use for colouring, pop in birthday party bags or turn into a DIY present for family and friends.

COTTON BUD PRINTING

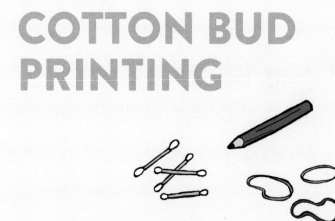

I find that the traditional plastic paintbrushes marketed for children do an okay job, but the result is always the same. The only variation in the style of painting comes from the thickness of the brush and the pressure applied to the surface. There are so many creative alternatives you can try which, dare I say it, may lead to better results. We've had a go at painting and printing with all sorts of objects and my favourite by far is using cotton buds. If you haven't tried this method of creating a picture using clusters of dots, I'm quietly confident you'll love it.

WHAT YOU NEED
• Poster paint
• A large pack of cotton buds (eco friendly are best, which use paper or bamboo sticks instead of plastic tubes)
• A few elastic bands or hairbands
• White paper, card or a canvas

HOW IT WORKS

1. Naturally there are any number of things you could paint, so to keep it really simple, I'll explain here how to create a field of flowers. However, when you've tried this out a few times, I'm sure you'll see lots of ways you can adapt the technique to paint other things!

2. First, you need to make your dabbers – the pseudo paintbrush made out of cotton buds. It is a good idea to make a few different ones as you can't wash the colours off like you can with a paintbrush (however you can wash them at the end and leave to dry so that they can be used again). However, do remember that you can use both ends of the buds to paint with. I tend to make three different sizes of dabber, using five buds for the smallest, ten buds for the medium dabber and fifteen for the largest one.

3. Tie your elastic band or hairband around the middle of the cotton bud dabber and twist the buds so that they splay outwards to create a flower-like shape. And don't worry if they're wonky. The idea here is lots of little dots on paper make a wonderful big picture and so this won't be noticeable. My top tip is to have a handful spare so that you can go back and add to your painting to get it how you want it to look at the end.

4. Set your paints up on a flat surface next to your paper or canvas and you are ready to go! I would first use one side of your smallest dabber with some green, which you can use to make a dotted stalk, or even swipe the paper to leave some green trails. You can then use your medium and bigger dabbers to dot round petal shapes or some tall pyramid shapes to represent hollyhocks, poppies or daffodils. Trees are fun to do with this method as the tiny dots mimic leaves really well. Toddlers can dab onto paper and easily achieve a meadow effect, with some grown-up help!

5. When you feel you've finished, grab your spare cotton buds and add in more individual dots if you like. You might also want to use a felt-tip pen to add lines or patterns, although this is entirely optional.

6. There are so many simple patterns that look breathtakingly good when done with tied-up cotton buds. Rainbows can look abstract in a beautiful way, a sunset image could take on new meaning, or a landscape inspired by a postcard or holiday snap could be fun to copy.

7. If you have older kids and have some colouring pages lying around, using a cotton bud to 'colour in' with lots of small dots is a lovely quiet activity to try and requires very little prep too.

SHORT OF TIME?

If you don't have cotton buds and want to give this a whirl, why not use your fingerprints to create some fingerprint art? The principle is the same and would be a great way to explore sensory play with younger kids. All you need to do is paint your child's forefinger with some paint, or let them dip their finger in some paint on a plate, and away you go. A flower shaped like a daisy is easy to make out of fingerprints, a yellow fingerprint can be turned into a bumblebee with a few black lines, and lots of white fingerprints on coloured paper would make excellent sheep!

PAINT-FREE MARBLING

Marbling is very rewarding – you get results quickly and they are quite unlike anything you can create by hand. What is unique about this art activity is that you never quite know what the end result will be. This sense of anticipation is great for kids to experience. When you've tried it out a few times, try not to marble everything in sight. It is tempting, but you may live to regret it!

WHAT YOU NEED

- Nail polish in a few different colours, the runnier the better

- A tub or mixing bowl of warm water, around half full. The nail polish will float on the water and so shouldn't damage the bowl, however I'd use something you don't mind getting a bit dirty.

- Small, hard, clean objects to marble such as a plastic pot, cup, coaster or candle. When you've done it once, I'm sure you'll see how it could work on other items you have around your home.

HOW IT WORKS

1. Put your bowl of water on a flat surface. Place some kitchen roll or an old cloth beside it to catch any drips and to lay your creations on to dry when finished.

2. Using the wand of the nail polish, swirl different colours of nail polish into the water. A few broad strokes, circles and dots is particularly good to get a varied pattern on your items.

3. Gather together the small glass or plastic items you don't mind experimenting on, and slowly dip them into the water and let the nail polish catch onto them. Help your kids to swirl them around so that you've gathered the nail polish on the sides – and there you go. You might want your kids to wear rubber gloves for this stage, just to keep little fingers away from the nail polish. My top tip is to try to roll any flat surfaces on the water first, rather than dipping in corners or points.

4. You'll probably need to add more nail polish after each dip, depending on how big the items are and how much nail polish they attract. Experiment with colour combinations and patterns on the water to see what effect this has on different surfaces.

5. Make sure you put your new creations on display. You might also like to take some close-up photos on your smartphone to really admire your masterpieces and to share with friends.

SHORT OF TIME?

Try shaving foam marbling, which is super simple. Spray the contents of a can of shaving foam into a shallow dish or baking sheet, add droplets of food colouring and swirl it around with a cocktail stick to create a pattern. Press a piece of paper gently on the top, letting it absorb the colour, and then carefully peel it back and scrape off the shaving foam with a spatula or dry cloth. Instantly, you'll have something ready to frame, draw on, cut up or use to decorate greetings cards.

MAGAZINE COLLAGE

This idea is inspired by a stranger who left a crate of interior design magazines out on the street near where I live, with a note that read 'for your arts and crafts'. I grabbed a handful, shoved them under the buggy and spent the walk home with my head spinning with ideas. Magazine or newspaper collaging is nothing new, but it's such an incredibly versatile activity and enables kids to be creative without having to draw a single line. It is all about making choices and showing your ideas on paper, without the fear of making a mistake or getting it wrong. And so rather than tell you how to do it, I'm going to give you three easy ways you can try it out to suit you and your kids.

WHAT YOU NEED

- Scissors – big ones for you and little ones for smaller hands if you have them
- A glue stick (we have several in our house, which tends to avoid arguments)
- A surface to stick on – this could be paper, the back of wallpaper or lining paper, cardboard etc.
- Newspapers and magazines. If you don't have any at home, you can usually find some by asking locally or seeing if friends and family have a stash. Depending on where you live, there might be local organizations who have some to give away. Free magazines from supermarkets or shops are also great.

HOW IT WORKS

Here are three collaging ideas which you can adapt as you see fit.

• DREAM HOME: Ask your kids to decide what their dream home would be like, leaving it nice and open for them to choose. Ideas could include the location (a desert island, a forest?), the type of building, the things they want inside their house, the colours they like, and so on. They could even choose a planet they'd like to live on, as there really are no boundaries.

• RESTAURANT: Ask your kids to create a collage of their dream restaurant and what it would serve! This would be particularly good if you have any cookery magazines or can get hold of some free ones from the supermarket. You could ask them to design a menu or even the concept for a restaurant if your kids are a bit older.

• SELF-PORTRAIT: I particularly like this idea as I think any activity that encourages kids to reflect on who they are is both meaningful and worthwhile. Ask your kids to draw either an outline of their heads or an outline of a body on paper. They then choose images and/or words that they feel attached to or in some way represent them. They might like to focus on their hobbies and interests, their favourite things, or their hopes for the future. Again, the more open you can make it, the better.

SHORT OF TIME?

Requiring less time and much less paper than the above activities, you can make a collage crown instead. Take a strip of paper that will fit if wrapped around their heads and encourage them to decorate it however they think would be fit for royalty. They could make a rainbow crown, sorting images to stick down by colour, or an ombré (where one colour blends into another colour) effect. Cuttings can stick up to make jagged edges or jewel shapes, and you can then use your crowns for dressing up, make believe or just to wear for fun.

LIFE DRAWING TWO WAYS

I know what you're thinking and I'm going to deal with that query right away. No, there is no nakedness involved in this. And yes, you can do this with your kids! This art activity is definitely more about relaxing and enjoying the process than producing an impressive end result. Here are two ideas, one drawing faces through a transparent surface and another drawing on each other's backs, which are perfect for a rainy day. I'm confident you'll have the resources for this activity and I'm also sure it will make you laugh out loud. Have fun, and try to take a picture or two of your family as you go, as you'll want to keep these moments as memories, even if you don't keep the drawings themselves.

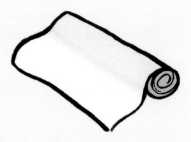

WHAT YOU NEED

- Something transparent to draw on. A piece of plastic that is roughly A4 in size would be ideal, such as a food container lid, the lid of a storage box, a square of plastic from the inside of a frame, a transparent document holder or even some plastic packaging. You could also do this activity on a window or glass door if you have somewhere suitable.

- Washable felt-tip pens – you don't need anything special, just avoid anything labelled permanent, like a Sharpie. If you're using a window or glass door, check first that the pen wipes off easily.

- Sticky tape, masking tape or Blu-Tack

- Sheets of plain paper

HOW IT WORKS

FACE LIFE DRAWING

1. Grab your piece of plastic and a felt-tip pen. It is handy to have a damp cloth nearby to clean the plastic when you need to, but this is not essential.

2. Sit on a chair facing another person. If your kids are drawing you, make sure they are sitting higher up so that they can reach your face, as they will be tracing the outline onto the plastic. Alternatively, sitting on the floor also works well as your kids can easily move around and kneel if they need to.

3. The person who is having their face drawn holds the plastic in front of their head and this frees up the hands of the person drawing.

4. The drawing can now commence! The aim is to draw the person's face as accurately as you can by tracing onto the plastic, and whilst this sounds easy, it is quite tricky and the results can be hilarious.

BACK-TO-BACK DRAWING GAME

1. In this drawing game, one person has a piece of paper stuck on their back and a piece of paper to draw on in front of them. Their partner does a drawing on the paper on their back, which they copy onto the paper in front of them. The idea is that you have to feel for the lines and try to recreate your partner's drawing on your back on the paper in front of you.

2. My kids find this hilarious, partly because they are both very ticklish, but also because rarely do the pictures mirror each other.

3. It is worth pointing out that you don't have to draw a picture. Younger kids could practise drawing shapes or letters. For slightly older ones you could try out words. If you do go for a drawing, you could give the person hints or clues to help them.

4. Whilst this activity involves two people primarily, you can also do it in a chain of people and see if you can get the same result drawn each time. It's actually quite a good ice breaker or team building activity, if you ever needed one of those.

SHORT OF TIME?

Blindfold drawing is incredibly fun and the sort of thing your kids can get on with while you cook dinner – I'm always on the hunt for activities that serve this purpose! Very simply, blindfold your kids with any suitable material you have lying around and decide on an image that they are likely to be able to draw, such as a cat, an ice cream cone and so on. Ask them to imagine the image in their heads, touch the edges of the paper so they know where to draw, and then off they go. For two or more kids, you could turn it into a competition, although the emphasis here is very much on having a good giggle.

RAISED SALT PAINTING

Raised salt painting really is a one size fits all activity, and when we've done it as a family it isn't always clear who is enjoying it more, me or my kids! I love watching the salt soak up the colour of the paint; in this sense, the resources do much of the hard work for you. The results of raised salt painting are quick, effective and will give those who are less 'arty' a boost of confidence. Just a quick warning, as you will be using salt, to make sure your kids know not to put it in their mouths and to keep any pets well away from your salt dish.

WHAT YOU NEED

- 500g table salt
- PVA glue in a squeezy bottle
- Liquid water-based paint or watered-down food colouring
- A sturdy painting surface: card, thick paper, paper plates or canvas
- Paintbrushes – ideally fine-tipped ones

HOW IT WORKS

1. Place your paper or card on a flat surface and use a pencil to draw the outline of a picture. Rainbows, cobwebs and snowflakes work particularly well for this activity. Take your bottle of PVA glue and gently squeeze a line of glue along the outlines you have drawn. Younger kids will probably need a bit of help with this.

2. An alternative to drawing a picture with the glue is to swirl the glue across your art surface in an abstract pattern. There is absolutely no pressure, and if there are blobs here and there, that just adds texture to the picture.

3. Now it is time to prepare your salt. I do this now rather than at the start to avoid little hands playing with it or knocking it over! Empty the salt into a small bowl or dish and grab a metal spoon (any will do).

4. Hold your glue picture just above your tray or dish of salt (which is there to catch the salt) and using the metal spoon, sprinkle a generous amount of salt over the glue, so that it is completely covered. Let the excess salt slide off the surface back into your tray or dish. Do this for the whole picture until all the glue is coated in a good layer of salt. Leave to dry – if you try to paint on the salted glue when it is still wet underneath, it will slide about. How long it takes to dry will depend on how thick your glue is. I find a few hours, so that it firms, is just fine.

5. Dip your paintbrushes into your paint or food colouring that has been watered down slightly. Slowly dab the paint onto the salt and watch the colours run away like magic in opposite directions! Try not to disturb the glue with your paintbrush and make sure to emphasize to your kids that they don't need much colour or pressure to make the salt change colour.

6. Leave your artwork to dry fully, which should take a day or so. But it is worth the wait, and at the end you'll have a wonderfully colourful, shimmery picture to admire.

SHORT OF TIME?

I'm a huge fan of cheap portable watercolour paint kits that you can buy, the sort that come in a plastic case or tin with a paintbrush included. Using one of these, I have a quicker, simpler version of raised salt painting which is ideal for keeping little hands out of mischief. Ask your kids to paint some paper lightly with water first, and then fill the paper by painting watercolours in an abstract pattern. Shake some salt across the painting whilst still wet and watch the salt soak up the colours. Their pictures will now look like a magical galaxy and your kids can go back and dab more colours in, on and around the salt to create something really special.

BUBBLES ON PAPER

There is something truly wonderful about an activity that is as enjoyable for grown-ups as it is for kids. This is one of those activities. Bubble painting is an oldie but a goodie. I can remember doing it when I was young, although a not so fond memory of sucking up the bubbles rather than blowing does linger still. The basic idea is that you blow into a coloured bubble mixture which creates a dome of shiny bubbles that make beautiful prints on paper. I particularly enjoy the uniqueness of each creation and the simplicity of the activity. Definitely one for a relaxed Sunday afternoon.

WHAT YOU NEED

For each individual colour you'll need:

- A tumbler, small bowl or plastic food container
- 1 tablespoon of water-based paint or food colouring
- 1 tablespoon of washing-up liquid
- Half a tablespoon of water

You'll also need:

- Straws to blow with – I've tried plastic, paper and metal straws and all work equally well
- Paper or card to print the bubbles onto

HOW IT WORKS

1. This can get a bit messy and so it's a good idea to set your bubble blowing supplies out on a flat surface, which is protected with newspaper or a cloth. Alternatively, this is a great activity to do outside if that is an option.

2. Make your bubble mixtures by adding the paint, washing-up liquid and water to your containers. Give them a good swirl with a spoon and try them out by placing a straw into the mixture and giving it a slow blow. If you feel it needs a bit more water, or the colour could be more vibrant, change the quantities accordingly.

3. This is the fun part! Get your kids to take their straws and slowly blow into each container of mixture. The bubbles should start to rise up and you want to keep going until there is a small dome rising from the top of the container.

4. As slowly and carefully as possible, lower your paper onto the cloud of bubbles above each container. The bubbles should make a gorgeous abstract print! You can layer up the colours as you wish and then leave them to dry.

5. I'm a huge fan of DIY greetings cards (as you will have probably gathered) and you can buy plain ones in bulk very easily. Your bubble prints would make a gorgeous decoration and one simple and effective way to do this is to cut a rectangle slightly smaller than the size of the card out of your bubble print paper, stick it down, and then with a black marker, draw a silhouette, letter, name or memorable date – and voilà, your card is ready!

SHORT OF TIME?

A quicker version of this is simply to pop a few drops of food colouring or a tablespoon of poster paint into a pot of shop-bought bubbles (or a few different colours into two or more pots for a multi-coloured effect), the sort that come with a bubble wand. Your kids can then enjoy blowing bubbles at paper to create a colourful print. It creates a more sparse effect than bubble blowing with a straw, but it is still a nice way to capture an activity on paper and would be great to do outdoors on a rain-free day.

WHIMSICAL ICE PAINTING

Don't let the word 'ice' lull you into thinking this is a warm weather activity. It really is something you can do all year round, and you can even theme it to suit any particular festivities or events with different colours and flavours! Ice painting quite literally means you'll be painting with ice, and there is something sensory and enchanting about whizzing frozen cubes of water across a surface. The focus of ice painting should be on enjoying what is a genuinely engaging, mindful and stress busting activity for all ages.

WHAT YOU NEED
- Ice-cube tray or mini muffin tray
- Wooden lolly sticks (preferable but not essential)
- Paper – the back of an old roll of wallpaper or lining paper works well
- Food colouring – either liquid or gel

HOW IT WORKS

1. Pour water into your ice-cube or muffin tray evenly so that it is nearly to the top. Add a few drops of food colouring to each cube of water, mixing carefully. Don't scrimp on the colouring, as you want the colours to be nice and vibrant on the paper.

2. Leave to freeze, ideally overnight. You have the option here of simply freezing the colourful cubes as they are and letting little hands use them as they are. Or you can leave them for an hour or so until they are starting to harden and then insert a lolly stick into each one.

3. When they are fully frozen, pop them out of the tray by running a little warm water over the back of the tray to loosen them. Put some paper on a Tuff Tray outside, or flat surface inside and get painting! The more the ice melts, the more colour will emerge and so your kids will be kept busy.

4. To bring an additional sensory element to this activity, you can add flavouring to the ice before freezing it and enjoy some lovely smells as you paint. We like peppermint mixed with green food colouring and lemon mixed with yellow. You can also make this seasonal by painting with particular colours, such as red and green during December, and adding in biodegradable glitter to your mixture.

SHORT OF TIME?

You can simplify this activity by actually painting blocks of ice! Fill some lunchbox-sized plastic boxes two thirds full with water and freeze. When solid, pop out and place on a tray, dish or inside a larger plastic box (they will melt and so you'll need something that will hold the liquid). There should be one block of ice per child, in an ideal world. Set out some ordinary poster paint and paintbrushes. They then paint the ice and, as it melts, they'll have a blank canvas to start all over again. And there's no need to wash your brush as the melting ice does that for you.

SEASONAL HANDPRINT TREES

The main resources for this activity are your kids' arms, hands and fingers, which will be used to make a tree shape on paper and can be coloured in to represent the different seasons. We have an apple tree in our garden and I dread to think how long I've spent staring at it through the kitchen window. I'm obsessed with how it changes from season to season. In the winter, it adopts a spooky skeleton structure of twigs and branches; in spring it sprouts a coat of thick white blossom; in summer the leaves are bright green and provide plenty of cool shade; and in the autumn the apples fall and the leaves slowly fade before disappearing entirely. The yearly cycle of a tree is one of nature's many miracles and making handprint trees is a lovely way to celebrate this.

WHAT YOU NEED
• Washable water-based paints
• Paper or card
• Paintbrushes

HOW IT WORKS
1. The first step is to draw around the hand and arm of your kids with a pencil. Ask them to place their forearm and hand palm downwards on a piece of paper or card, with their fingers spread out, and trace around it carefully. Their forearm will be the trunk of the tree and the handprint will form the branches.

2. If you have time on your hands (no pun intended!), do this first step four times on different sheets of paper to represent the four seasons, or you can always pick your favourite season to begin with.

3. Fill in the tree's trunk and branches with brown paint so that you have a solid tree structure in front of you, or cut out some card in the same shape to add texture and variety to your picture.

4. You are now going to use your fingerprints to create the leaves. Decide which season you are going to do first, and which colours you will be dabbing on the paper. White and pink prints signify the blossom of spring really well; orange and browns can represent autumnal leaves; blues and whites could signify a wintery scene; and bright shades of green could help illustrate summer. Place some paint on a shallow plate and dab away!

5. A lovely way to develop this activity would be to listen to Vivaldi's *Four Seasons* while you're doing your paintings. There is a different piece of classical music for each season, and each one is around ten minutes long. The music can be a talking point and it would be great to play a particular season as you are painting it!

SHORT OF TIME?

For something quicker and less messy, try some hand or fingerprint painting on cling film. Set out some newspaper or if like me, your shower curtain, dot a piece of paper with splodges of paint and then cover this with cling film, taping it firmly to your newspaper. Alternatively, you can place your paper inside a zip-lock plastic bag for even less mess. Let your kids then 'paint' the paper by pressing, swiping and moving the paint around underneath the cling film with their fingers. Carefully peel back the cling film and voilà, a multi-coloured abstract wonder, which can be drawn on when dry. You might want to choose blue and white paints to create an underwater scene or orange and yellow paint to create a swirly sunset.

TRIED AND TESTED CRAFTS

Don't flick to the next chapter just because you see the word 'craft'. Stick with me so I can explain. I know even the mention of the 'c' word sends some parents running for the hills and I don't blame you. But crafting can be fun, enjoyable and straightforward. It is all about picking the right craft, doing it at the right time, having an open mind and not worrying about the outcome. If it is wobbly, splodgy and uneven, it is all evidence of some great family time together. Teaching kids creativity gives them a life skill and crafting is a brilliant way to foster this. It is so easy to write off some crafting as a failure if it didn't turn out right, but the learning is all in the process, not the result. So rid yourself of your crafting worries and give some of these tried and tested activities a go. You never know, you might even enjoy yourself.

GLOW IN THE DARK DREAM CATCHER

Involving your kids in making their own dream catchers is not only a fun crafty way to spend time together but it also puts them in charge of an aspect of their bedtime and will add a bit of magic to the bedtime routine. By cutting out the middle of a paper plate and weaving some string or wool through, you will quickly have a magic web to decorate as you like. Using some glow in the dark paint or stickers makes this a great addition to 'lights off' at bedtime.

And anyone with kids knows that going to bed can be far from straightforward, so anything to make that process a bit better is always going to be a win. Having a dream catcher provides a great talking point about why sleep is so important and how our lovely dreams will be caught and kept safe.

WHAT YOU NEED

- Paper plates – one per dream catcher
- String, ribbon, wool, twine or traditional packing string
- Washable paint and/or felt tips
- Craft accessories for decoration: pom-poms, craft feathers, beads, glitter glue, sequins, etc. Or use dry macaroni pasta left plain or painted.
- Glow in the dark stickers and/or glow in the dark paint

HOW IT WORKS

1. Take your paper plate and fold it in half. Cut out the middle of the plate by cutting a semi-circle close to the rim of the plate. When you unfold the plate, you should be left with a nice neat circle cut out.

2. Now, imagine your plate is a clock, and punch some holes roughly where the twelve numbers would go. These will be used for threading string.

3. If you want to paint your plate, do it now and leave it to dry. Or, if you want an easy life, like me, your kids can use felt tips or pencils to decorate the plate. Add stickers, glitter, sequins, whatever you fancy, so long as you don't cover the holes!

4. Now is the string bit. First, take three 20cm pieces of string (same size as the width of a sheet of A4) and tie them to three holes next to each other, which will be the bottom of the dream catcher. Tie a double knot, leave most of the string hanging down and then decorate by adding beads, tying on feathers, or dry macaroni pasta, left plain or painted. Make sure you secure the string at the bottom so that your items stay put.

5. This is the bit my kids love the best. Threading! Take a long piece of string, around a metre to be on the safe side, and knot to one hole. I would go for what would be 12 o'clock on your plate. Thread the wool across the plate, upwards, sideways and diagonally to create a web. Don't forget to thread through the bottom three holes too.

6. When you feel your web is complete, tie a knot in a hole of your choice and cut off the excess string. You can glue it in place too if you have a strong glue to hand.

7. Now it is time to get your glow on! If you're using glow in the dark paint, I recommend painting the string by dabbing it on the web that you have created, and also around the plate itself. If you have glow in the dark stickers, fix them wherever you think they look best on your dream catcher.

8. Using the hole at 12 o'clock, use a short piece of string and tie a loop at the top so that it can be hung on the wall. Or alternatively, you could stick it on any suitable surface using Blu-Tack.

SHORT OF TIME?

Dream wands are a quick alternative to a dream catcher. All you need is a twig or stick to decorate, and before you know it, you have a magic wand to get rid of any bad dreams and to magically keep all the good ones safe. Decorate your stick with ribbons, wrap wool around it, stick on any craft items you have to hand, or even use nature from an outside space. A bit of a cardboard box could easily be cut to make a star to stick on the top.

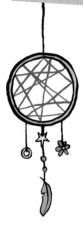

AIR DRY
CLAY MEDALS

Air dry clay is so easy to use and I've included a quick recipe below, if you fancy making your own. It is safe for little (or big!) hands to mould and dries in the air so no messing around with hot ovens. Medals are quick and easy to make using the imprint of a coin (any will do) and can make great gifts, jewellery and dressing-up items to boot. Medals exist for so many different reasons and so this is the craft activity you can go back to again, again and again. Enjoy.

WHAT YOU NEED

- 1kg pack of air dry clay – or make your own using the recipe below
- Coins – a selection of shapes and sizes would be ideal
- Paints or felt tips to decorate (not essential)
- Ribbon or material that can be cut for wearing the medal around the neck

RECIPE FOR DIY AIR DRY CLAY

- •1 cup cornflour
- •1 cup craft glue such as PVA glue
- •1 tablespoon lemon juice
- •1 tablespoon vegetable oil

1. Mix all the ingredients together in a non-metal bowl.

2. Microwave for 30 seconds.

3. Stir the mixture together (it will look lumpy).

4. Pop back in again for another 30 seconds.

5. Mix and knead in your hands, using more cornflour as needed, until you have a soft dough, ready to use.

HOW IT WORKS

1. Roll out your clay on a non-stick surface until it is around 2–3mm thick. Baking paper is a good way of making any chopping board suitable for this activity.

2. Now cut out circles in the clay. You can use a cookie cutter or make a small template to cut around. My top tip is to cut around the base of a toilet roll tube as it is just the right size and chances are you'll have one lying around somewhere!

3. Using a sharp pencil, skewer or matchstick (unlit of course), punch a hole in the top of the medal, big enough to poke through the ribbon or material cord, and a good few millimetres away from the top, so that it will be strong when hung.

4. Now take your coins and slowly but firmly press them into the centre of the circles of clay. Carefully lift them off and you'll be left with an impressive imprint that looks very real indeed! And you don't need to be limited to just coins. Your kids may enjoy searching for items that would make a good print in the clay – the possibilities are endless.

5. Leave your clay to dry. This will take up to 24 hours. When they are dry, you can paint and decorate as you like. We've had lots of fun using gold and silver paints to make ours as real as possible, but they look just as good left plain.

6. Thread your ribbon through the hole and tie a knot, making sure the loop is big enough to easily take on and off.

7. You can have fun making medals for family or friends and they do make great presents. Instead of a coin imprint, use the nib of a sharp pencil to write 'Best mum/dad/sister/brother/friend ever', or create some family awards of your own. You could even go as far as to have certificates to match and host your own awards ceremony together!

SHORT OF TIME?

Air dry clay does take time to dry and so if you fancy something quicker, simply replace the clay with card and follow the same steps as above. You can either punch a hole for the ribbon or stick it between two circles of card, or to the back of the circle itself. Your medallions can be decorated with anything, from wrapping paper to whatever is in your recycling bin, and this would be a great way to engage your kids in thinking about how to make something out of things they already have.

CARDBOARD CUT-OUT SHADOW WRITING

This activity needs nothing more than some cardboard, scissors and a sunny day. By simply cutting out letters or shapes, you can make shadow words – but make sure you take some photos, as I guarantee they'll be the sort that end up in a frame. Watching my kids chase their shadows in the sunlight brings me deep joy, and I have real nostalgia about the beauty of shadow puppets silhouetted against a wall from when I was little. And shadows only exist when there is a light and there is something deeply special about that.

WHAT YOU NEED

- Cardboard – the bigger and thicker the better. It is good to plan ahead and save up delivery boxes. My local convenience shop always has spare boxes and this might be another option.

- Scissors or a craft knife

- A smartphone to take a picture

- A sunny day – I realize you can't plan this, but you can prepare your resources in advance for when the sun does pop out from behind a cloud!

HOW IT WORKS

1. Lay your cardboard out on a flat surface and using a pencil, draw the outline for the words or numbers you have chosen. This could be a memorable date like an anniversary or birthday, your kids' names or initials, the word 'love' with a heart for the 'o'. It really is up to you.

2. If you have one big piece of card, you can try to get your cut-outs on one piece. Alternatively, if you have smaller pieces of card, you can do individual letters and ask each family member to hold them up. Get your kids involved in this stage, planning how big the letters should be and how best to draw them out.

3. Cut along the lines carefully and keep them as clean as possible. Any fuzzy bits of cardboard left hanging around may be visible in the shadow. There is no need to decorate the card. I'd go as far to say that it is more slick if you don't, but I'll leave that up to you.

4. Next, and this is the trickiest bit, wait for the sun to shine! It doesn't need to be a hot day, just a very bright one with direct sunlight that would ordinarily create a shadow. When the moment has arrived, go outside and hold the card up and let the shadow of your words or numbers silhouette against the floor or a wall.

5. Take a photo – as many as you need! Keep them, frame them, stick printouts on birthday cards – there really are so many ways to showcase this snapshot in time.

SHORT OF TIME?

If you have Lego or Duplo at home, there is a great way of making a very simple shadow theatre with a piece of paper and a torch or lamp! Build two towers of bricks towards one side of a traditional brick mat and using some Blu-Tack, attach the paper to the towers, like a screen. Position your torch or lamp so that it is shining at the paper. From the same side as the light, your kids can use figures, bricks or any other small toys to create a puppet theatre for whoever is sitting on the other side of the screen.

MAGICAL GLOW JAR

This gorgeous activity repurposes any old jar destined for the recycling bin into a magical world in the palm of your hand. By coating the inside of the jar with watered-down craft glue and some biodegradable glitter or paint and slotting in a silhouette and a battery-operated light, you'll have a magical scene that will inject wonder into any child or grown-up! It isn't complicated to do, and with a tiny bit of forward planning so that you have the resources on stand-by, you can turn any rainy afternoon into one of wonder and surprise.

WHAT YOU NEED
- A medium-sized glass jar with a lid
- PVA glue and paintbrushes
- Biodegradable glitter and/or poster paint
- Card and black paint or a black felt tip
- An LED tea light

HOW IT WORKS
1. The first step is to paint the inside of your jar with glue. For the first coat, empty approximately 3 tablespoons of glue and 1 tablespoon of water into a small pot or ramekin. Mix until you achieve a watered-down consistency.

2. Pour the mixture into the jar, pop the lid back on and shake it around until the inside of the jar is coated. Tip the excess glue back into the ramekin (you might need it later) by holding it upside down. Clean and dry the lid and leave to one side.

3. Whilst the glue is wet, you are going to apply the glitter to it if you have some, so that you coat the inside of the jar. Add the glitter in bit by bit, rotating the jar as you go. You can get an

even coating by popping the lid back on and giving it a vigorous shake. If you'd rather use paint, wait until the glue is dry and then paint the inside of the jar with some watered-down paint of your choice. You don't need too much, just enough to give the glue a bit of a tint in the colour of your choice.

4. Next, you need a small silhouette or two to place inside the jar. Let your imagination run wild! This works really well with a magical creature such as an elf, fairy or dragon! You can print off an image and use it as a template or draw one of your own onto card. Check it is big enough to fit inside your jar and paint or colour your silhouette black.

5. When the glue and glitter feel dry to touch, you can pop in your silhouette and stick it down or prop it up inside the jar. If you want to add in more silhouettes, go for it. Alternatively, you could think about what other small items would look good with light shone on them – a small twig looks very much like a tree, for example!

6. Now it is time to decorate the outside of the jar – if you want to. I like to wrap twine around the top of my jar to give it an earthy feel and I've seen brilliant creations that have stuck objects on top of the lid itself – small stones, leaves or twigs look great.

7. Switch on the LED tea light, pop it inside the jar and then enjoy the magic in a dark room. It really is a magical sight.

SHORT OF TIME?

You could also make a coffee filter luminaire jar. Lay out a few paper coffee filters and let your kids paint them with swirls and shapes using watercolours or watered-down poster paint. Leave to dry and then tear up into small pieces. Cover the outside of your jar with PVA glue and layer up the pieces like a mosaic, making sure they overlap to cover the jar. When finished, cover all of the stuck-on filter paper with more PVA glue to secure the layers. When it is dry, pop an LED tea light inside and you're done!

REUSABLE FACE PAINT BOARD

This activity was such a hit with my kids, I was a bit annoyed I hadn't tried it sooner! I gave them each a laminated board with a face on it which they then decorated with washable felt-tip pens, which could then be wiped off. It was so simple, cheap and easy to do and occupied them for much longer than I expected. It is also portable – you could take this out and about and you'd have an engaging activity with minimal props. Here are two simple ways that I found work best.

WHAT YOU NEED
- Cardboard – I use the plain side of a large cereal box
- Sticky back plastic
- Wool or string
- Washable felt tips, or paints and fine paintbrushes
- Optional: stickers

HOW IT WORKS
1. Take a piece of cardboard that is A4 in size or bigger and lay on a flat surface. Draw the outline of a head and shoulders with a pen or marker so that it takes up most of the space. Next draw the outline of some eyes, ears, a nose and a mouth.

2. Now you need to laminate your card using the sticky back plastic. Cut out two pieces that are slightly bigger than your cardboard. Peel a little of the backing away from the plastic, stick your cardboard in place, and slowly peel back the rest, smoothing it down as you go. Repeat for the other side of the card. I tend not to include my kids in this step!

3. You are going to cut out some small holes in the laminated cardboard so that you can push through wool or string for the hair. Your kids can cut it, plait it, tie it up and so on, which is great for littler ones to develop their fine motor skills. Make three evenly spaced holes, around half a centimetre in diameter, around the top of the head. Take a handful of string or wool and cut into lengths of around 25cm. Poke as much as you can through each hole, and tie in a big knot on the other side, or tie with a hairband if easier, to keep in place.

4. Now you have your finished piece, lay out your washable felt tips and paints and fine paintbrushes (and stickers if you want them) and you can start decorating! Your kids can design face paints, superheroes, turn them into a celebrity or just do a self-portrait.

5. To reuse the board, simply wipe clean with a damp cloth and replace the hair with new lengths of string or wool.

SHORT OF TIME?

Why not print out pictures of family or friends and cover them in sticky back plastic or place inside a plastic wallet for your kids to decorate with felt-tip pens! If you don't have a printer, try one of the companies that let you print free photos for a small delivery charge. Your kids might like smaller photos to work on rather than something big and popping some in your bag on the go makes the activity super portable.

DIY DOUGHNUT PIÑATA

If you've never had a go at bashing a piñata, fear not, because now is your chance! A piñata is a container usually made of card, clay or papier-mâché, filled with toys or sweets, suspended from a height and then bashed until the contents fall out. It's a great party game; however, you certainly don't need to wait for a party to have all the fun. I've chosen a doughnut-shaped piñata here as it is easy to hang and you can make it largely out of what's in your recycling bin.

WHAT YOU NEED

- Cardboard – the more you have, the bigger your piñata can be
- Sticky tape – the stronger and thicker the better
- String, ribbon or twine
- Colour: You can choose to paint your piñata or cover it in tissue paper, party streamers, wrapping paper, etc.
- Doughnut sprinkles: You can use coloured paper, felt, fabric, card, stickers or anything else that will make sprinkles on your doughnut.

HOW IT WORKS

1. On your largest piece of card, draw and cut out two large circles that are the same size. I would draw one, cut it out and then use it as the template for the other one. These are the front and back of the doughnut.

2. Take a bowl and draw around it in the centre of each circle. The size of bowl you need will depend on the size of your doughnut ring! Cut out the smaller circle in the middle to make the hole of your doughnut.

3. Now you need to join the two large circles together. Take some card, approximately 15cm wide, and stick to the edge of one of the circles with your sticky tape, bending around the circle shape as you go. Don't worry if you don't have enough to go all the way round, just add more and stick it to the last piece until the circle is complete. Do the same for the inner circle, so that you have a ring shape that will be complete with the larger circle placed on the top.

4. Decide on your treats and put these into the base with the sides. These can be anything, from edible goodies to small toys you already own, or even petals or leaves from the garden so that they burst out like confetti.

5. Take your second cardboard circle and attach on the top of the base with the treats inside which should be on a flat surface. Use tape to attach it on the outside as you can cover this up later.

6. Now decorate your piñata doughnut however you fancy, although pretend sprinkles look great. Party streamers are helpful for this stage as you can wrap them round and round the doughnut case you have made. You can also paint it, collage with paper of any sort or just leave it, particularly if your cardboard is brown.

7. Leave to dry before looping a large piece of string through the small hole. Now you can hang up your doughnut and attach it to any location, although make sure you choose a spot where your kids will have the space to bash.

8. Ask your kids to get a stick or a wooden spoon each and take it in turns to bash the piñata, maybe three bashes per person per go. Whoever manages to break open the piñata can be crowned the winner!

POM-POM
WALL HANGING

It is no secret that I'm a pom-pom fan and I had no idea how easy it is to do it yourself until I gave it a go. This activity will teach you how to make a pom-pom from scratch and then attach it to a stick which can then be hung from your wall. They make great inexpensive gifts and without any glue or paint being required, make minimal mess and so quick to clear up afterwards. You can buy pom-pom makers, and you can buy them ready-made, but using some wool and cardboard, I'll talk you through the simple steps so that you and your kids can add another 'we can make that' string to their craft bow!

WHAT YOU NEED

- A ball of wool – any colour, shape or size, although my top tip is to go for rainbow-coloured yarn, so that you get automatically multi-coloured pom-poms
- A kitchen fork
- String
- A stick or twig

HOW IT WORKS

1. The first step is to wind your wool around the fork – a regular four-pronged fork is best. Place your wool across the fork, halfway down the prongs, leaving about 10cm spare at the end. It is worth pointing out that you are making small pom-poms for this activity rather than the big fluffy ones you sometimes see.

2. Wrap the wool repeatedly around the prongs of the fork until you have a really thick ring of wool in place – about 5mm in depth.

3. Cut the wool from the ball and tie the two loose ends to each other nice and firmly and trim off the excess thread. Cut a short piece of wool, around 20cm long, and simply thread it through the middle prongs of the fork and around the middle of the ring of wool. Pull tight and do a double knot to keep it secure.

4. Pry the wool off the fork by pushing it off the prongs. Take a pair of scissors and cut through the two loops of wool either side of the knot in the middle to hold it together. Fluff it out in your fingers and you should have a little pom-pom in your hands.

5. Give your pom-pom a little haircut with the scissors to make it neat and uniform before having a go at another one. It really is so quick and easy. Ideally you will make around six pom-poms, but it really is up to you.

6. Now you want to attach your pom-poms to your stick! Take three lengths of string or wool, maybe around 20cm each and tie onto the stick, spacing them out evenly. You will have a hole in the middle of your pom-pom and the aim is to thread the string that is hanging from the stick through the pom-poms. If you have a bodkin needle, that might be handy, but I just use my fingers.

7. Finally, snip 30cm or so of wool or string and knot near each end to the stick. Hang where you like and make sure you and your kids stand back to admire your work!

SHORT OF TIME?

Draw and cut out the shape of a cloud on card, ideally around A5 size. Next, draw the same shape 2–3cm smaller inside and cut that out, so you have a cloud-shaped ring. Take some wool and stick down on the card – it doesn't matter where – and slowly wrap the wool around the cloud until you have covered all of the card. Wrap the end of the wool around another strand and tie a small knot or glue it in place so that it is hidden. Cut a piece of string and make a loop which you tie to the top of the cloud or stick in place. And, before you know it, you'll have a beautiful cloud, ready to hang.

MILK BOTTLE DINOSAUR HEAD

When you've done this, you'll never look at a plastic milk bottle again in the same way. I've tried this out a few different ways using different sized milk bottles and below you'll find my best version so far. By cutting the bottle at key points, and sticking masking tape down strategically, you'll show your kids how to turn trash into treasure by turning an ordinary milk bottle into a rather realistic dinosaur head.

WHAT YOU NEED
• A regular two-litre plastic milk bottle with a lid
• Masking tape (my preference is FrogTape)
• A small piece of cardboard – any will do
• Paints and paintbrushes

HOW IT WORKS
Note: You don't have to follow my instructions to the letter as you will start to see your dinosaur emerge in a few snips and should feel confident to own your design, with the help of your kids, of course!

1. I'm sure this is obvious but it is important to properly clean and dry your used milk bottle, as you don't want any unpleasant odours further down the line!

2. Take the lid off (keep it for later) and lay your milk bottle on a flat surface, handle facing up and hole towards you. Cut along each side to the bottom of the milk bottle so that you have two halves that open and shut easily.

3. Cut off the end of the bottle where the milk comes out – this should be easy to do with the milk bottle cut in half.

4. Cut around the handle part of the bottle in an oval shape and cut some small slits around the edge of it so that you can easily place this on top of the other side of the milk bottle. Fix in place with masking tape and pop strips of more masking tape over the handle so the gap is filled in – this is where the eyes of your dinosaur will be.

5. Fill in the hole from where you removed the handle area with a piece of cardboard. Use masking tape on the outside and on the inside to make it secure enough to be painted.

6. Now take the bottle neck pieces you had and cut them in half. Stick two at the front of the top half of the bottle to act as nostrils and two further back higher up to be eyelids for your dinosaur.

7. Now take the bottle lid, cut it in half, and stick down with glue or masking tape underneath your eyelids.

8. Time to make your dinosaur teeth! There are a few different ways to do this, but I prefer the simplest version, which is just to cut zig-zag teeth all around the top and bottom halves of the milk bottle. You can also shape the jaw line of the dinosaur at this stage if you want to, going up a bit at the back for effect!

9. Your shaped head should be complete, and so now the challenge is to paint it to look as realistic as possible. Poster paints do work on milk bottles and masking tape, or acrylic paint is excellent if you have some. This point is also an opportunity for your kids to do some quick research to check what colours they should use and any dinosaur features they can paint on.

10. Have fun playing with your newly created dinosaur heads, and if you do decide to chase each other around your home, snapping as you go, just remember that the teeth actually can be quite sharp!

SHORT OF TIME?

There is a much simpler version of this which you and your kids can do together very easily, and doesn't involve any masking tape. Take your clean, dry, empty milk bottle and cut it in half the other way round, from the base to around 10cm from the lid either side. On the same side as the bottle handle – which will be the brow of the dinosaur – cut out two nostrils towards the front. Now cut out teeth along the cut edges, and your dinosaur is ready to decorate however you see fit.

FLASHLIGHT AQUARIUM

If you are looking for an activity that can make even the most cynical youngster go 'wow', then this optical illusion is for you. Using the power of paper, pens and a plastic bag, you can make a magically lit-up scene, simply by colouring on the plastic bag and using white paper underneath to illuminate it. We love to go for an underwater scene, but it works brilliantly for any colourful landscape with recognizable features, such as a farm or beach scene. This is a really simple craft activity that requires no prep or fancy resources. I hope you enjoy it as much as we do!

WHAT YOU NEED
• White paper
• Black paper, or painted black card
• A transparent plastic bag, such as a zip-lock bag
• Semi-permanent coloured markers such as Sharpies

TOP TIP: Have multiple bags and pieces of paper as the chances are, your kids will want to do this again and again!

HOW IT WORKS

1. Place your sheet of white paper into your plastic bag and cut to size if it is a little bit big. It should fill the bag, ideally.

2. Draw a picture on top of the plastic bag in markers such as Sharpies that work well on plastic surfaces and don't smudge. This works really well if you draw a scene. My kids' favourite is an underwater scene with coral, jellyfish, sand, crabs, sunken treasure and so on. Colour in as much as possible as the more colour there is, the more effective the end result.

3. Take the white paper out of the plastic bag – it should be totally clean as you have drawn on the bag itself. Take your black paper and place it inside the plastic bag, cutting to size if needed, so that you can no longer see the drawing on top of the plastic bag.

4. Now go back to your white piece of paper. Draw the shape of a torch on the paper with a triangular beam of light coming out of it. Colour in the body of the torch but leave the beam of light plain white. Cut the torch out of the paper so that it is like a large funnel shape.

5. Here is the magic part! Tell your kids to pretend to turn on their torches, and holding the handle, insert the plain white beam of light into the plastic bag on top of the black paper. The scene you drew should be magically illuminated, without a battery or light switch in sight!

ICE CREAM PARLOUR PLAY DOUGH

No matter what age kids I have round for a playdate, play dough is a firm favourite. I'd actually say it is my go-to activity, come rain or shine. Here is my favourite TWO-INGREDIENT recipe that makes a gorgeous silky creamy texture that can be scooped easily to make pretend ice cream and smells divine. Pop the ingredients in your next food shop and you're good to go!

WHAT YOU NEED

- 500ml hair conditioner – the cheaper the better, and a fruity scent is ideal
- 700g cornflour
- Food colouring – three different colours is ideal
- Real ice cream cones, or card to make pretend versions
- Optional decorations: buttons, sequins, real sprinkles, beads, stickers, cotton wool (for marshmallows), pom-poms, foil scrunched up into small balls, etc.

> TOP TIP: If you can, buy cornflour in bulk as it keeps for ages and is incredibly handy to have for all sorts of craft recipes.

HOW IT WORKS

1. Take out a large mixing bowl, pour in the cornflour and make sure there aren't any lumps. Add about two thirds of the conditioner and mix with a wooden spoon. Slowly add in the rest of the conditioner, stopping when you have a lovely creamy mixture that isn't too sticky. If you do add the conditioner in too quickly, no problem. Just add in a bit more cornflour.

2. Divide the dough roughly into three bowls. Add a drop of food colouring to each bowl. I go for pink, yellow and blue and add it very sparingly as a little goes a long way.

3. You can leave your play dough ice cream in the individual bowls if you like. We've also had a lot of fun putting it in a leftover ice cream tub! You'll find that the quantity of dough will fit into most 1-litre (or more) ice cream tubs, which is handy. My kids like to put the three colours next to each other, a bit like Neapolitan ice cream, as it looks so pretty.

4. On a tray, lay out your ice cream accessories. If you are using real ice cream cones (our preference), just make sure you explain to your kids that whilst they can usually eat these, they shouldn't if they have the play dough mixture on them. If using foil balls, beads or buttons or any other small items, just keep an eye on littler ones to make sure they don't end up in mouths.

5. Give each of your kids an ice cream scoop and away you or, more accurately, they, go! They can mix and match flavours, layer colours up, decorate with different toppings, serve them to each other, their dolls, have an ice cream party, create an ice cream menu with pictures . . . there is just so much fun that can be had. And the good news is it will all smell amazing because of the conditioner. I hope you love it as much as I do.

SHORT OF TIME

If you need a quick calming activity, I really recommend 'Coconut Cloud Play Dough', which like the recipe above only needs two ingredients: coconut-scented hair conditioner and cornflour. The quantities are the same as the main activity. Use your coconut cloud play dough to create clouds for toys to bound across, or make different cloud shapes on a piece of blue paper, and even give them special names.

WHIZZY EASY SCIENCE

I'm no scientist. And yet, despite not having studied science for over twenty years, I still harbour a deep love for the whizz, pop, bang of an experiment that does something you really don't expect. I am always on the hunt for activities that will spark curiosity in my kids and encourage them to want to ask questions and learn, and conducting easy science experiments at home is a fantastic way to do this. To keep life simple, most of the experiments here involve ordinary household ingredients, however a couple do involve some slightly more unusual items including hydrogen peroxide and glycerine. But don't let that put you off. In a few clicks, you'll find what you need online, and the results, I promise you, will be worth it.

ROCK CANDY SUGAR CRYSTALS

My kids are constantly asking for sweets, despite the fact we rarely have any at home. There's no judgement from me about sugar consumption, none whatsoever – we tend not to have them simply because I tend to eat them! This activity, which involves growing your own sugar crystals, is a nice halfway house between sweeties and science. I am confident that you will have all the ingredients for this wonderful table-top experiment lurking in your kitchen, so it doesn't require much, if any, planning ahead – always a win.

THE SCIENCE BIT: By dissolving sugar in hot water, you create what is called a supersaturated solution. When you dip string into this solution, you give all those sugar molecules bouncing around something to cling to, and in the process grow rock candy sugar crystals that are good enough to eat.

WHAT YOU NEED
- A clean glass jar (jam jars are ideal)
- 4 cups white sugar (caster or granulated)
- Pencil
- String
- Optional: food colouring

TOP TIP: It takes up to a week for the crystals to grow. Prepare your kids for this. The excitement we've had, dashing downstairs before breakfast to see how they have grown, is totally worth it, though.

HOW IT WORKS

1. Pop your jar on a flat surface. Now take a pencil, tie a piece of string around it and rest it on the top of your jar. You want the string to hang nearly to the bottom of the jar but not quite, so cut to size as needed.

2. Run the string under some warm water to wet it and then dip or coat it in some sugar and leave to one side.

3. Pour one cup of water and four cups of sugar into a saucepan and heat it up until nearly boiling and all of the sugar has dissolved.

4. Carefully take the saucepan off the heat and pour the mixture into the jar. If you have food colouring, add a few drops and stir with a spoon until the colour of the water is how you want it.

5. Lower the string into the jar and let it hang in the water, resting the pencil across the top of the jar.

6. Store somewhere safe and check in on it regularly. You can take the string out of the water and pop it back in whenever you like. After around 5–7 days, you will have glittery sugar crystals in the colour of your water, which look enchanting, and are very, very sweet!

7. If they aren't played with or eaten straight away, you can store your candy crystals in an airtight container. Check the use by date on the packet of sugar you used to know how long you can keep them for although in my experience, they can keep for a very long time!

ONE STEP FURTHER

Another way to make this is using pipe cleaners instead of string. Hang a pipe cleaner from a pencil, in the same way as the string, but this time, make different shapes with the end of the pipe cleaner that go into the sugar, such as a circle or a zig-zag. Notice how the forming sugar crystals cling majestically from your new shapes!

RAIN IN A JAR

If it actually is raining outside, why not give your kids a quick and easy demo on the kitchen table of your own little rainstorm? By popping some shaving foam (clouds) on top of water (air) in a jar and dropping food colouring on top (rain), you'll have an experiment in density that your kids will love. When we did this, we listened to music which was linked to the weather, starting with 'It's Raining Men', you know, just for fun.

THE SCIENCE BIT: Clouds are made up of billions of droplets of water vapour and when they are heavy enough, gravity pulls them down as raindrops. This experiment is a simple model of that process and is both fun and fascinating to try.

TOP TIP: Ask your kids beforehand to write down or tell you what they think is going to happen. Ask them again at the end what they noticed happening and why they think that is. Boom. Learning.

WHAT YOU NEED

- A can or bottle of shaving foam
- A jar, the taller the better
- Food colouring
- A pipette, spare medicine syringe or any kind of dropper

HOW IT WORKS

1. Prepare your rain first, by filling a ramekin or cup with water, around half full. Add in your food colouring until the water is your desired colour. The darker the colour, the more visible your rain will be.

2. Take your jar and fill it two thirds full with cold water. This is going to be your air and will hold up the shaving foam on top.

3. This is the bit my kids love best – squirting the shaving foam onto the water in the jar. If your kids haven't had the pleasure of squirting out foam or gel that expands into foam from a container before, maybe let them have a go on some kitchen towel first, before taking aim at the jar of water!

4. Now is the magical bit where you add in your rain! Using your pipette or syringe (why we have several Calpol syringes in our cutlery drawer, I'll never know), let your kids fill it nearly full with the coloured rainwater and then drip it slowly onto the cloud.

5. Keep slowly adding droplets until the cloud begins to get heavy with the coloured rainwater and it starts to drop through underneath. We normally have cheers in our house when this happens! Keep going until your cloud is saturated and can't take any more.

6. We are never happy doing this just once in our house and tend to do this over and over again with different coloured food dye, making multi-coloured rain. We've also had a rain challenge where my two kids both have a jar each and whoever is first to get a droplet underneath is the winner.

BOUNCY BALL EGGS

Bouncy eggs are a discovery I made relatively recently and are ridiculously easy and incredibly fun. All you have to do is place a raw egg in vinegar and leave it for a few days to transform into a squidgy, bouncy ball. The vinegar is acid and dissolves the shell, however the egg inside isn't affected as the white membrane around keeps it safe. You can play games with your eggs, rolling them around and seeing what happens when dropped (as the egg inside is still raw). And if you have a smartphone, filming them move in slow motion is truly fascinating.

THE SCIENCE BIT: Vinegar is an acid and the shell of an ordinary chicken egg is made up of calcium carbonate. The vinegar moves through the shell of the egg and dissolves the calcium but cannot get through the membrane, which leaves behind the rubbery membrane so that the egg is bouncy.

WHAT YOU NEED
- An egg
- A glass tumbler or jar
- White vinegar

TOP TIP: Try to be patient – the longer you leave your egg, the easier it will be to remove the shell and have the best bouncy egg.

HOW IT WORKS
1. Take your egg and carefully place it in your glass or jar.

2. Fill the glass with white vinegar so that the egg is fully submerged. If you're making more than one egg at a time, just make sure you have enough vinegar to cover them all fully.

3. Put your glass or jar in a safe spot, cover it with foil and make sure it isn't in direct sunlight. Leave the egg to soak for around 72 hours. When the shell of the egg begins to go transparent, it's a sign the egg is ready to be played with.

4. Let your kids take the egg out of the glass and rinse it under water, allowing the shell of the egg and the white film to come off. You will be left with an egg that feels rubbery to touch and is slightly translucent, so that when you hold it up to the light, you can see the yolk in the middle.

5. Let your kids test out the egg in their hands and ask them questions about what it feels like. It's worth pointing out that the egg inside is still raw and so any damage to the outside could result in an egg explosion!

6. Now you can have fun bouncing your egg and seeing what happens. I recommend starting by dropping your egg approximately 10cm above a flat surface. Have a tray or some newspaper ready to catch any spills that may occur.

7. We've enjoyed making this into a game by taking it in turns to drop an egg to see if it goes splat! Start at 10cm as described above, and have everyone try dropping it from a couple of centimetres higher each time. The suspense is thrilling!

ONE STEP FURTHER

Whilst this game is good enough on its own, there is an additional step that you can try for even bouncier eggs. If you have any bouncy eggs left, place them in a bowl of golden syrup and leave for around 10 hours (or overnight). Your egg will shrivel up, but fear not, this is part of the process. Now place your egg in a bowl of tap water and squeeze in some food dye. After another 6 hours, you will have your bouncy egg back, but this time brightly coloured and really very rubbery!

ELEPHANT'S TOOTHPASTE

I'm going to go out on a limb here and say that I guarantee your kids will go 'wow' when they do this experiment. When I've done it with my own kids, as soon as we've finished they ask to do it all over again. By combining a few simple ingredients, you're going to create expanding foam that's so big it looks like toothpaste for elephants exploding out of a tube, hence the name. The only ingredient you may have to source is hydrogen peroxide, which is widely available in shops and online and often used as an antiseptic. Plus, you can use it for many other science experiments and so it certainly won't go to waste.

THE SCIENCE BIT: Hydrogen peroxide is broken down by an enzyme found in yeast, called catalase. This reaction produces oxygen and water. It happens very quickly in this experiment, meaning that the oxygen gas gets caught in the soap, causing lots of tiny bubbles and foam.

TOP TIP: Get your kids to put on any science-related fancy dress they have, as it creates the feeling of a laboratory at home. If you have any rubber gloves, do ask your kids to pop those on too. You can call it dressing up but it will protect little hands against the ingredients.

WHAT YOU NEED

- 1 teaspoon of dry active yeast
- Hydrogen peroxide at 6% (I used some from a brand called Kusuri but there are lots available to buy online)
- Food colouring
- Washing-up liquid
- A small measuring jug
- A tray or plastic tub
- A jug or large jar
- Washing-up gloves or rubber gloves

HOW IT WORKS

1. First of all, make a quick and easy yeast solution by mixing 1 teaspoon of yeast with 2 tablespoons of warm water in the small measuring jug to make it easy to pour. Encourage your kids to give it a good stir until it is all mixed in, and then leave to one side.

2. Next you are going to prepare the area for your magical elephant's toothpaste to explode! Place the jug or jar you will be using on your tray or in your plastic tub. We do this experiment in a washing-up bowl which keeps all the mess in one place and can be quickly poured into the sink when finished! Get your kids to put on the gloves at this point so that they can pitch in with the next step.

3. Carefully pour in around half a cup of hydrogen peroxide into your jug or jar and add a few drops of food colouring on top. Next pour a tablespoon of washing-up liquid on top and give it a quick swirl to mix them all together.

4. Now this is the REALLY fun part. Pour your yeast solution from the small measuring jug into the mixture inside your jug or jar and take a big step back! Instantly, you'll see foam rapidly expand and flow over the top of the vessel and onto the tray or tub. It will be streaked with the shade of your food colouring, which makes it look a little bit like stripy toothpaste. Whilst it is not unsafe to touch, I would keep little hands away unless they are protected by rubber gloves.

BEST BUBBLES EVER

Let's be honest. When parents think about bubbles, the first thing that springs to mind are those tiny party bag bottles with the plastic wands. Even though they can be useful, in general I am not a fan. Not only do the contents invariably end up on the floor but, in my experience, trying to use them so often leads to tears and frustration.
And that is just the grown-ups! This activity is the exact opposite of that. Below is my tried and tested formula for the biggest and best bubbles ever plus incredibly easy ways to make giant bubbles and rainbow bubble snakes, which are both seriously fun.

THE SCIENCE BIT: Bubbles are made up of three layers. There is an outer and inner layer of the bubble, made up of soap molecules, and in between those is a thin layer of water, or so I'm told. Bubbles usually form spheres and the reason for this is that it has the smallest surface area for a given volume of air, letting it float about.

TOP TIP: Make your bubble mixture the day (or more) before you want to use it, as the bubbles will be stronger. If you can, make a large batch and decant into spare bottles or jars with lids so that you are bubble ready at any time! Also, a potato masher is a great bubble wand.

WHAT YOU NEED
- 1 litre of warm water
- 250ml of concentrated washing-up liquid
- 4 tablespoons of vegetable glycerine (which is easy to buy online – we use the brand Naissance)

HOW IT WORKS
It is a good idea to make your bubble mixture before you want to play with it and I tend to make mine the day before I need it, minus my kids. Pour a litre of warm water into a container and add the concentrated washing-up liquid and glycerine carefully. Stir very slowly and carefully as you are trying to avoid creating bubbles. Leave to stand in a safe dry place overnight

BUBBLE SNAKES
1. Take a plastic drinks bottle and cut it in half around the middle. Both small and large drinks bottles work for this, so use whatever you have, or experiment by using different sizes.

2. Slide a sock over the exposed end of the bottle and secure with an elastic band or hair bobble, so that it is taut over the end of the bottle.

3. Decant some of your bubble mixture into a shallow dish and, if you want to, add a few drops of food colouring and swirl around. Just remember that food colouring can stain!

4. Dip the sock end of the bottle into the bubble mixture and then blow through the neck of the bottle. A magical snake-like formation of bubbles will appear at the other end and you can carry on dipping and blowing until your bubble mixture is used up.

GIANT LOOP BUBBLES

1. Looping string around two sticks that you can find outside or on a walk is a great way to create large bubbles really easily. So the first step is to find two sticks, the longer the better, or you could use some dowel.

2. Take your string and measure around a metre in length, although this doesn't have to be precise. Knot the string to one end of each stick.

3. Now cut some additional lengths of string and knot to the main piece of string between your sticks in a U-shape, so that they are hanging down in loops. I tend to go for two big loops and cut 50cm of string for each, but you could make a few smaller ones if easier. Make sure that your U-shaped loops of string are knotted tightly to the main string, as this is likely to lead to better bubbles.

4. Decant your bubble mixture into a shallow dish to dip your string into (we use a Pyrex roasting dish which is roughly A4 size). Slowly immerse your string, swirl around a few times, and then whirl your arms around in the air and watch the bubbles fly!

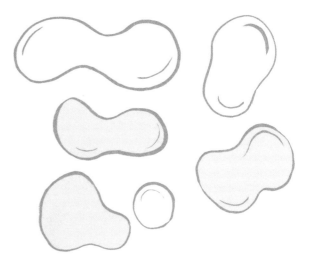

SHOOTING VINEGAR ROCKETS

This experiment is a real thrill. By repurposing a plastic bottle and a few store-cupboard ingredients, you can make a vinegar-powered rocket which will shoot into the sky much higher than you might expect. As such, it is essential to do this experiment outside. Once when we tried it out, our rocket shot up as high as our house! With that in mind, there are a few safety bits and bobs to consider, but don't let that put you off. The excitement of this experiment will enthral your kids and spark a real curiosity for how things work.

THE SCIENCE BIT: Combining bicarbonate of soda and vinegar creates a reaction which produces water and carbon dioxide gas. This builds up inside the plastic bottle and places pressure on the cork, popping it off and causing the bottle to blast into the air.

TOP TIP: Use freshly opened vinegar as old vinegar can lose its acidity and means the experiment may not work quite as well.

WHAT YOU NEED

- An empty plastic bottle (500ml or 1 litre)
- A bottle of white vinegar
- 1 or 2 tablespoons of bicarbonate of soda, depending on your bottle size
- 3 pencils
- A cork that will fit in the bottle neck
- Paper for decoration
- Kitchen roll
- Sticky tape

HOW IT WORKS

1. With your bottle upside down, use sticky tape to attach three pencils to the sides, evenly spaced apart. The flat end of the pencils should extend below the bottle top by a few centimetres, so that the bottle is held in place upside down when the pencils are placed on a flat surface.

2. Decorate your bottle with a few rocket fins at the bottom around the pencils and a paper cone on the top, which you can make by rolling up a triangle of paper. If you want to decorate your rocket more than this, just be mindful that you want it to remain light so it can shoot into the air!

3. Turn your bottle upright and pour in vinegar until it is one quarter full. Take the cork and make sure it fits into the bottle. Don't push it in too tightly.

4. Now take your bicarbonate of soda and measure out 1 tablespoon for a 500ml bottle and 2 tablespoons for a 1-litre bottle onto a piece of kitchen roll. Carefully roll it up so that it is fully encased, a bit like a sweet in a wrapper.

5. Take your rocket and your wrapped-up bicarbonate of soda outside. Find some level ground on which you can place your rocket and ensure that you have space to step back at least four metres when you launch your rocket into the air.

6. The next step must be completed by an adult. Turn the bottle so the neck is facing upward. Pull out the cork and push in the wrapped up bicarbonate of soda. Now replace the cork but not too firmly so that it can take off but also not too loose as you don't want anything to fall out. Turn the bottle round and place it down on your level ground.

7. Whoosh! Your vinegar bottle rocket should lift off into the sky when the bicarbonate of soda and vinegar combine and the pressure pushes the cork out. Do keep an eye out for where it lands, although it is unlikely to be far from your launch pad. If your rocket doesn't take off, the cork might be in a little too tightly. If this happens, loosen the cork a bit and take a step back, or take the cork out carefully as if opening a bottle of champagne and repeat the experiment again, which should take minutes now that you have your rocket ready!

ONE STEP FURTHER

Why not try out a rocket race? Your kids could design and make their own rockets and then launch them at the same time to see whose stays off the ground the longest. Alternatively, try experimenting with different sizes and shapes of bottles to see which ones are most successful and go the highest.

RAINBOW OOBLECK

Oobleck sounds happy. Even saying it makes me smile. And rightly so, as this little gem of an experiment only requires two main ingredients, needs no prep at all, and can lead to hours of gorgeous sensory play. Oobleck is a bit like slime, but messier and with different properties. But where did the name come from, I hear you ask? Well, look no further than the Dr Seuss book *Bartholomew and the Oobleck*, where a strange green goo fell from the sky onto the kingdom below.

THE SCIENCE BIT: Oobleck is an example of a non-Newtonian fluid, which means it is neither a liquid nor a solid but benefits from the properties of both. When you pour it, it looks like a liquid, but when you put pressure on it, it acts like a solid.

WHAT YOU NEED
• 2 cups cornflour
• 1 cup water
• Food colouring

TOP TIP: Have extra cornflour on hand so you can add some more if your mixture becomes too runny or if you want to thicken it up. And fear not, Oobleck does sound like a disaster to clear up, but it washes off easily with a bit of soap and water. If it does get on any non-washable surfaces, leave it to dry and then sweep or vacuum it up.

HOW IT WORKS

1. Pour your water into a bowl, and slowly add the cornflour, mixing as you go. It will feel very lumpy and will stick together to begin with. Your kids can start by mixing with a spoon but will soon find it tricky to stir. At this point, they can roll up their sleeves and use their hands. The aim is to get a mixture that feels like a solid as well as a liquid.

2. The Oobleck is ready when it still feels slightly lumpy to the touch but can be made smooth with your hands. Transfer it into to three smaller bowls. Add a few drops of food colouring to each bowl to get your desired colour, but be careful with little hands as you probably don't want them to get stained.

3. With your three bowls of Oobleck ready, you can play with it however you see fit. We love to pour all three bowls into a baking or pie dish and let the colours start to swirl together. It is fun to poke and move the mixture around and your kids can experiment by drawing shapes, letters and numbers into the mixture and trying to build things, only to see them collapse soon after.

4. There is something very calming about playing with Oobleck, especially when you take a handful and squeeze it really tight in your fist, letting the liquid ooze out and the solid remain in the palm of your hand. This might be a good activity for kids who need a way to relax or distract them from something bothering them. It can be just as good for adults to play with too, for the same reasons.

ONE STEP FURTHER

To make your Oobleck even more magical, you could choose to add in some biodegradable glitter. Or you can easily make your own 'eco glitter' by collecting petals and leaves, leaving them to dry and then cutting them up into really small pieces before storing them in a jar. The petals mixed in to the Oobleck add an extra sensory dimension to this activity which would be particularly good for toddlers to experiment with.

SOLAR BOX S'MORES

I discovered s'mores whilst on my honeymoon in America and felt cheated that I hadn't had them sooner. They are a popular campfire treat made from marshmallow and chocolate sandwiched between two biscuits – yum! The trick to make them extra delicious is to melt the marshmallow, which warms the chocolate and makes taking a bite heavenly. In the steps below, I'll show you how to make your own solar oven, which on a sunny day is the key to making this delicious treat.

THE SCIENCE BIT: Your solar box will be trapping the sun's energy so that the air becomes hotter inside the box than outside of it, like a mini greenhouse. The heat will enable what you place inside to become cooked.

WHAT YOU NEED
- A medium-sized closed cardboard box – a shoebox, delivery box or pizza box all work well
- Aluminium foil
- Cling film
- Sticky tape
- A stick, skewer, ruler or knitting needle
- Sharp scissors or a craft knife
- A bar of chocolate – any will do, including dark/vegan
- Marshmallows – any will do, including vegan
- Crackers or biscuits that are slightly sweet – we use digestives

TOP TIP: The best time to heat up your solar oven on a sunny day is between 11am and 3pm, when the sun is at its highest.

HOW IT WORKS

Making solar box s'mores can be best divided up into three stages. The crafting involved in making the oven, the heating up of the oven, and then the cooking of the s'mores when they are inside the oven. Oh, and eating them too, of course!

MAKE THE OVEN

1. Take your box and seal down all the sides with tape. Next you need to make a new lid or flap on the top of the box. To do this, take a craft knife or sharp scissors and cut along three edges of one of the large sides of the box, around 2–3cm in from the edge. By only cutting along three sides, your flap can open and close easily.

2. Now you need to cover the inside of the box with aluminium foil and this is a great stage to involve your kids. Give them a glue stick and dab it all over the inside of the box, including the inside of the lid/flap which opens.

3. Take your foil and cut it into pieces roughly the size of each side of the box. Now get your kids to stick them down so that the inside of the box is all silver and shiny. It helps to smooth the foil down if little hands are clean and dry.

4. The next step involves creating an airtight window so that your oven traps the sun's energy. You do this by lifting the flap and covering the opening with two layers of cling film. Tape it down tightly, allowing it to overlap the edges if you like, so that it is sealed shut.

PREHEAT THE OVEN

5. Take your solar box outside and ask your kids to find a really sunny spot. Use your stick, ruler, skewer or knitting needle to prop open the lid of the box so that the sunlight is shining in through the cling film and reflecting off the foil inside the lid and into the oven.

6. Leave the box outside for about an hour so that the sunlight can go through the plastic and heat up the air inside.

COOK THE S'MORES

7. Take your s'more ingredients outside to the box with more cling film and sticky tape. Peel back the cling film lid and let your kids place however many biscuits comfortably fit inside. On each biscuit, place a marshmallow. Traditionally the chocolate is put on first, but marshmallows take longer to melt and so this way round works best.

8. Reseal the lid with the existing cling film or add more so that your oven is once again enclosed. Leave the box oven with the lid propped up in the same position, allowing the light and heat to slightly melt the marshmallow. This could take up to an hour and your kids can keep checking and tell you when they think it's ready!

9. The final stage is to add the chocolate. Take off the cling film and pop a square or two of chocolate on top of each gooey marshmallow, then place a biscuit or cracker on top, creating a sweet sandwich.

10. Close the cardboard lid and leave in the sun for a few minutes so that the chocolate can melt a bit. You don't need to worry about the light coming in at this stage as the inside of the box will be nice and warm. When ready, lift out your s'mores and take a big bite. Enjoy!

ONE STEP FURTHER

If your kids enjoyed this and want to try it using different ingredients, you could try melting some cheese on crackers, or if you're feeling really adventurous, try cracking an egg onto the foil to see if it cooks. I would advise popping down a fresh sheet of foil inside the box after each go, or you could use a damp cloth to give it a wipe.

BREAD IN A BAG

Hold on. Wait. This is supposed to be the science section of the book. Ah yes, but baking bread IS science. The yeast that goes into bread to make it rise is, in fact, a single-cell fungus. Yum! And before your kids panic about eating fungus, don't forget to tell them that the yeast dies off when you cook the bread, so there really is nothing to worry about! For anyone who fears the difficulty of making bread, this is the recipe to try, and for anyone with kids who don't like getting their hands messy, the bread is made in a bag, so problem solved.

THE SCIENCE BIT: This recipe uses fast action yeast, which is made up of small hard balls of yeast to help the dough to rise. The yeast allows fermentation to take place, which is where the yeast eats the sugar and gives off carbon dioxide gas bubbles. These get trapped in the strands of the dough and kneading the dough helps the bubbles to increase, meaning the dough rises.

TOP TIP: This bread recipe is delicious with real butter, particularly when the bread is slightly warm, allowing the butter to melt. If you have some butter, take it out of your fridge at the start so that it's spreadable by the time the bread is baked.

WHAT YOU NEED

- A large zip-lock bag
- 375g plain flour
- 3 tablespoons granulated sugar
- 7g sachet fast action yeast
- 1 ½ teaspoons salt
- 230ml warm water
- 3 tablespoons olive oil

HOW IT WORKS

1. Take your zip-lock bag, open it, and place it inside a bowl so that the base of the bag sits in the base of the bowl. Fold down the edges of the bag over the sides of the bowl so that the inside of the bowl is covered by the bag.

2. Add in approximately one third of the flour together with the sugar, yeast and warm water. Let your kids give the contents of the bag a quick stir to combine the ingredients.

3. Leaving the bag in the bowl for now, squeeze out any air inside the bag and reseal it. Leave the mixture for approximately 15 minutes.

4. It is now time to add a few more ingredients, so open the bag again, using the bowl as a base, and tip in another third of the flour, together with the olive oil and salt. Take the bag out of the bowl and get your kids to squidge it around inside the bag.

5. When these ingredients are roughly combined, add in the last third of flour to the mixture, close the bag and continue to let your kids have fun massaging the dough, safe in the knowledge the plastic bag is keeping this relatively mess-free.

6. When the bread mixture looks combined and no stray lumps of flour remain, take it out of the bag, using a spoon or spatula to help you, and knead it on a clean surface for around ten minutes. If your mixture is sticky, add a smidge more flour. If it is too floury

you can add a few drops of water to loosen it up. Kneading the bread is the number one job for your kids here, so let them have fun with it – stick on some music in the background to keep them motivated.

7. Cover your dough with a damp cloth and leave for around half an hour. This will let the magic science bit happen. Whilst the bread mixture is proving, preheat your oven to 190°C so that it is hot when you are ready to put the bread in.

8. When the time is up, uncover the dough and shape the bread as your kids would like. Place on a baking tray sprinkled with flour, or just pop it inside a loaf tin.

9. Your bread should bake for about half an hour. Always do the tap test on a loaf of bread to check it is cooked– this simply means tapping the bottom of the loaf and if it sounds hollow, it is ready.

10. Leave the bread to cool on a cooling rack. Don't rush to cut it as you risk it crumbling apart, plus it will be incredibly hot. Whilst it is cooling, get any toppings ready that you might like to try, although as you'll see from my top tip, I think a good lashing of butter is all you need.

ONE STEP FURTHER
This simple recipe makes fantastic rolls. All you need to do is divide the mixture into balls just before the proving stage and bake for around 15–20 minutes. You could also experiment with different flavours your kids might like, adding in sundried tomatoes or olives to make a savoury bread, or chocolate chips before proving, to make your bread more of a sweet treat!

RED CABBAGE WIZARDRY

I seem to be the only person in my house who likes red cabbage and so we often have some left over. As a result, I was really keen to try this experiment as it put my leftovers to good use! My kids were so excited to see the colour of water change in front of their eyes and dashed around the house to find things they wanted to test. This little experiment really sparked their curiosity and turned a rainy afternoon into one full of wonder and wizardry!

THE SCIENCE BIT: Red cabbage juice contains a natural pH indicator that changes colour when you add an acidic solution to it. The pigment that causes the colour change is called flavin, and when very acidic solutions are added to it, it will turn red, more neutral solutions will turn it purple, and more alkaline solutions will turn it a greenish yellow.

WHAT YOU NEED
• Half a red cabbage
• 4 regular drinking glasses
• 4 different testing solutions: lemon juice, washing powder, bicarbonate of soda and vinegar all work well.

HOW IT WORKS

1. Take the half red cabbage and chop it up into small chunks – you don't need to be precise. Put the chopped-up cabbage into a medium-sized saucepan and leave to one side.

2. Fill your kettle with around 500ml of water. When it has boiled, pour it into the saucepan with the cabbage and put over the heat to simmer. It is best an adult does this stage.

3. Simmer the cabbage for about ten minutes. This is enough time for the water to take on the purplish colour of the cabbage. Ask your kids to keep a timer. Turn off the heat and leave to cool.

4. Take a colander and place over a jug. When the water in the saucepan has cooled down, pour the contents into the colander, so that the purple water goes into the jug. The cabbage is now cooked and can be saved and eaten – delicious with butter and a pinch of salt!

5. Now transfer the cabbage water equally into the four glasses. There is no need to measure exactly, just do it by eye. If your kids have a steady hand, they can complete this step with your guidance.

6. Lay out your testing solutions and ask your kids what colours they expect these to turn the water. Now let your kids take it in turns to add in small amounts of the solutions to see how the water changes colour. I'm certain there will be a 'wow' moment, even two or three!

TOP TIP: If you have any rubber gloves, you might want to pop them on as purple cabbage can stain easily. I can be quite clumsy so I also wear an apron.

LET'S GET PHYSICAL

It is a Sunday afternoon. It is 4pm. Your plans have been rained off. Your kids are bouncing off the walls. And you've already told them there is no more TV for the rest of the day. Sound familiar? If so, this chapter is for you. Here are ten great physical activities that have worked for me when my kids have needed to burn off some energy. Plus they are really, REALLY fun. However, the need to get kids moving goes beyond just filling the time. I don't need to tell you how important it is that kids are active, or about the health benefits of physical activity. You know that already. It's often just hard to know where to start. With that in mind, let's get going.

SECRET AGENT LASER CHALLENGE

Do your kids laugh in the face of danger? Do they believe they are indestructible? Well, today is their lucky day. Their mission, should they choose to accept it, is to channel their inner secret agent and retrieve treasure by navigating a laser obstacle course without tripping the wire. By very simply attaching string or wool to walls or doors, ideally along a corridor or narrow space, you will create a labyrinth that your kids can climb through and play around for ages.

Hard to picture in your head? Imagine an action film with a scene in a museum where an important artefact is about to be stolen. You know those neon green lines that are supposed to protect the exhibits and trigger the alarm? Well, that's the inspiration here! Although hopefully your kids won't set off any alarm bells whilst doing it!

TOP TIP: Ask your kids about their favourite spy film or TV show, and quiz them on what makes a good spy, what might be the best and worst parts of being a spy and what spies might need to look out for. Create a backstory before you start – spy name, spy costume, spy mission and so on.

TREASURE!

WHAT YOU NEED

- String or wool (any type), ideally 10m or more
- Treasure: a basket or box and objects to put in it
- Sticky tape or Blu-Tack

HOW IT WORKS

1. Decide where you want your laser challenge to be. Involve your kids in scoping out the best place to do their mission. A hallway is ideal and any narrow space will work. However, if you have enough string and can summon the energy, you can go for a whole room. The main thing is to have a start and end point.

2. Part of the mission is to collect treasure and return it to where it belongs. Ask your kids to do a quick treasure hunt around your home and place the objects in a box or basket at the end of the challenge. Bear in mind that your treasure needs to be reasonably easily carried back through the maze, so big objects will be trickier!

3. Now it is time to construct the maze – it is easier than you might think. Tie your string to something at the start to keep it in place, such as a banister, door knob or cupboard handle – anything, so long as it doesn't move. Now zig-zag your string from anchor point to anchor point – these can be anything your string can be tied around, or you can use sticky tape or Blu-Tack to fix it in place.

4. Your kids can now begin their mission! The aim of the game is to use their agility to weave in and out of the maze to collect the treasure. They can try to do this in one go or over a few goes. You could even have two teams. Make sure you remind them they can't touch the laser string.

5. If you fancy adding in an extra challenge, you could plant your treasure at strategic points throughout the maze, add in obstacles like cushions or boxes, or tell your kids to do it with their hands clasped together.

ANY WEATHER MINI GOLF

There is a huge Jurassic-themed mini golf course near me, where giant dinosaurs tower over you as you play, complete with sound effects and plenty of prehistoric-looking foliage. I've definitely used these 'distractions' as an excuse for my poor golfing performance, although I don't think anyone bought it! Traditional golf is a game where you try to get balls into eighteen different holes across a large area in the smallest number of shots. Mini golf focuses mainly on the putting bit of the game, where you are close to a hole and use the club to knock the ball in.

Mini golf isn't just reserved for elaborate courses or holiday resorts. You can easily create mini golf challenges in your home or garden using a few household items. I'm going to tell you how to design, build, play and keep score for your own mini golf course. Mini golf is not only easy and entertaining for all ages, it will inject a bit of healthy competition at home too.

TOP TIP: Put some sweets or treats wrapped up inside the cups that will be the holes you aim for in the game. This works wonders for motivation!

WHAT YOU NEED

- Golf clubs or croquet clubs (or any equivalent item)
- Golf balls or other small balls
- Masking tape
- Plastic or paper cups (I use IKEA kids' cups and wash them thoroughly afterwards)
- Pen and paper

Household items to build your course (pick and choose from whatever you have):

- Books to build a ramp
- Toy train tracks or plastic tracking for a ramp
- Tin cans to act as obstacles
- Empty cardboard boxes
- Toilet rolls to act as tunnels
- Soft toys and teddies to position cups against

HOW IT WORKS

1. To get your kids to buy into the activity, get them to help you design and map out the space and how it will work. They can write it down on paper, draw a picture, move objects around, or just tell you what they think. No idea is too big or small and if they are lacking in inspiration, send them for a hunt around your home to find props to use.

2. The next challenge is to build your course. I would suggest having a few different 'stations'; however, the important thing is to go with what your kids have chosen to do! If you do need some pointers, here are a few suggestions:

    TEDDY BEAR 'PUTTNIC': Position teddy bears – as many as you want – in a circle formation and wedge a plastic cup next to them facing inwards, or use some masking tape if needed. The aim of the game is to stand in the middle of the circle and hit as many holes in one go as you can.

DOLL DIRECTIONS: Gather as many dolls as you have into an open space. Position them across the space and prop their arms up so that they are pointing in the direction you want the game to go. Wedge or stick a cup on or near the dolls to aim the ball into. Your kids then follow the direction of the pointed arm to the next hole.

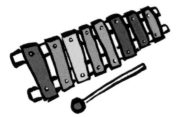

HIT THAT NOTE: This idea uses any musical instruments you may have at home to literally hit a note when playing mini golf. Use a xylophone as a musical ramp, position any jingle bells against a wall that you have to aim for with the ball as part of the course, or prop up cymbals (we have small toy ones) so that when the ball hits them they make a noise.

SKI SLOPE SLALOM: Use some tin cans for this one, or anything else you find in your food cupboard that you don't mind being potentially bashed by a child with a stick! Place your cans out in a line, spaced 30cm or so apart. A bit like a ski slalom, your kids have to putt the ball in and out of the tin cans, without it rolling away, and get it into a cup positioned at the end.

3. The aim of the game here is to have fun. However, challenge and competition is a great motivator for many kids and so keeping score is a great idea. Mini golf normally involves nine challenges and the aim is to get the ball into the hole in the fewest number of hits. You can download your own mini golf scorecards online, or easily make your own by drawing a simple table with columns for each challenge and then rows for each person taking part. Add in how many hits everyone took and award prizes to the lucky person who got through with the fewest putts.

HOME-MADE SPORTS DAY

I dreaded sports day at school. I wasn't very good at running or sitting on hot grass and waiting my turn, plus the 1980s wasn't very kind when it came to gym kits! However, I loved the actual games themselves and having rediscovered their joys during lockdown with my own kids, sharing them here is a quick reminder that sometimes we already know what to do, and just need a nudge. I'm sure the games don't need much explaining and so here are my top five from which you can pick and choose.

> TOP TIP: Make medals in advance using either air dry clay or more simply with cardboard – see the Tried and Tested Crafts section.

WHAT YOU NEED
- Eggs
- Wooden or metal spoons
- A tie or strip of material
- A football
- Sponges
- Buckets
- Tin cans
- A tennis ball or bean bag

HOW IT WORKS

Your sports day can have as much or as little structure as you like. If your kids are used to sports day at school, they may have their own views on activities, the order, how and where to do them. What does need to be clear is the starting line for each activity, to make sure it is fair.

EGG AND SPOON RACE: The simplest and in my view the best! All you need is a start and end point to your race, a wooden or metal spoon and a raw egg. The excitement of the egg cracking is great fun but messy, and so I wouldn't blame you if you decide to go for a partially cooked one.

THREE-LEGGED RACE: This is great for family bonding as you'll quite literally be tied together. Two people, ideally of similar height, stand beside each other and have their nearest legs tied together with a tie. The challenge is then to walk quickly without falling over. You can try to time how long it takes to do one lap and whether you can improve your three-legged technique to get quicker over time.

BALL BETWEEN THE LEGS: This is an alternative to the traditional sack race as I'm pretty certain hessian sacks aren't a household staple, and it is just as fun! All you need to do is place a ball between the knees of the people taking part and complete the race without dropping the ball, by hopping or waddling. It is fun to take part but perhaps funnier to watch.

SPONGE BUCKET RACE: You'll need two buckets for this race, one half full of water and one empty. The aim of the race is to use a sponge to soak up as much water as possible from one bucket, run, and then squeeze it into the empty bucket at the other end. The person who moves the most water in a given time frame is the winner, or you can choose to do it in teams if you have enough people.

TIN CAN ALLEY: This is a simplified version of bowling where you use nine tins (ideally empty) to create a pyramid and then use a ball or beanbag to attempt to knock them down. Setting it up on a table or raised surface makes it much easier when aiming. Take it in turns to see how many you can knock down each time. I particularly like the inclusive nature of this game as it can be done sitting down if needed.

I WENT TO THE . . . MOVING MEMORY GAME

? ? ?

WIGGLE YOUR EYEBROWS

This game is so quick and easy, it almost doesn't warrant a full description. But because it is so quick and easy, I want to make sure you know exactly how it works, so you can whip it out and play anytime, anywhere. If you remember playing the game 'I went to the shops and I bought . . .' in the playground when you were little, this is a physical version of that, where you have to remember your own and other people's actions and then complete them accurately in a sequence.

TOP TIP: Take a photo of this page and keep it saved on your phone for when you are stuck out and about and need a quick idea with zero resources. You can play it in the park, waiting in a queue or during a kids' playdate. It is super versatile.

WAVE

HOP

WHAT YOU NEED

Genuinely nothing. Comfortable clothing would be a bonus and any prizes or treats for the person who remembers the most would be nice.

HOW IT WORKS

1. You need at least two people to play this game. Two people can stand facing each other to play and three or more people can stand in a circle to play. Tell each person participating to think of a few different actions they can do with their body and to keep it a secret for now!

2. Choose someone to start. They will begin the game by saying 'I went to the . . .' They can choose where they went – it could be the shops, the park, a soft play, the beach and so on. They complete the sentence by saying 'and I got a . . .' and then do their action. They then pass it to the next person in the circle or their partner if playing in pairs.

3. The next person says 'I went to the . . . and got a . . . ', and they have to say the same place as the previous person and do their action, and this time, add in an additional action of their own.

PAT YOUR HEAD

4. This pattern then gets repeated between the pairs or around the circle for as long as you can keep going! The first person to forget or make a mistake has to sit down and the person who remembers the most can be the winner.

5. Older kids might like more of a challenge and so if you have a small ball, you can throw this randomly around a circle instead of going round in sequence. This makes it harder to remember and the kids have to stay alert as they never know who is going to be next!

TWIRL

SHAKE

SIDEWALK CHALK CHALLENGE

I realize sidewalk is an American word, but there is something about it that oozes cool to me, in a way that the word pavement or patio simply does not. So don't worry if you are reading this and thinking, where is my sidewalk? You don't need one. All you need here is some chalk and ground on which your kids are allowed to scrawl. The aim of the activity is to draw out physical challenges on the floor that you then follow to get moving. You could also do this indoors if you have a big enough space and your floors allow, but personally I feel this is one for the great outdoors.

WHAT YOU NEED

- Jumbo chalks are ideal. Smaller chalks work, but are harder to use.

OR MAKE YOUR OWN CHALK PAINT:
Mix together half a cup of cornflour with the same amount of baking powder. Add in droplets of water until you get a smooth paint/paste mixture. Add a few drops of food colouring and stir to make the colour of your choice – you can divide up the mixture to make different colours. Grab a paintbrush and away you go.

HOW IT WORKS

1. This is great to plan with your kids first, so have a team meeting and decide on what sort of physical moves and actions should be included. A great way to get the conversation going is to ask your kids what they might have seen in a park or school playground, what their favourite shapes are or how they could include numbers.

2. Go to your desired spot and get your chalk ready. To make smaller chalks easier to use, you can either crush them and mix with water to create a paste-like paint, or prep your homemade paint, if using. Driveways and patios are great for this. Depending on where you live, you may be close to an open space that allows chalk to be used. Please do check before you commit paint to floor, so as not to break any rules.

3. There are so many possibilities for how you create games on the floor, so to make life easy, I've chosen five that my kids particularly loved.

    HOPSCOTCH: A classic but still a great crowd-pleaser

    MAZE: Use your chalks to mark out a square or a circle, on the floor, the bigger the better and then fill with a pattern or lines to create a maze that you have to walk or tip-toe through to get from one side to the other.

    ALPHABET HOP: Write out the letters of the alphabet and put a circle around each one, about 30cm apart. Call out words and get your kids to hop about to each letter to spell them out.

    SHAPE INSTRUCTIONS: Draw simple shapes such as squares, circles and triangles, and draw arrows on the edges of the shapes so that your kids have to jog around in the shape formation.

    SNAKES AND LADDERS: Draw ladders for your kids to jump up and snakes for them to run down. If you have some dice, you could even draw out a board and play the game in full!

ARGH! YOU'RE STANDING ON QUICKSAND

I'm always on the hunt for activities that I can quickly set up when I sense a tantrum might be on its way, or there is yet another request for TV. Don't get me wrong: screen time is great in moderation, but it's always handy to have an easy alternative up your sleeve. This activity is a variation on the game 'the floor is lava' and the idea is that you have to keep moving whilst not touching the floor, as it has turned to quicksand! The more you shout this at the top of your voice, the better! It is also great at the end of the day to help your kids burn off any excess energy before bedtime.

WHAT YOU NEED
Objects that will act as stepping stones: cushions, foam pads, bean bags, pieces of paper or cardboard, books, rugs, place mats etc.

HOW IT WORKS
There are two ways we like to play this, but the aim of the game in all instances is to stay off the floor aka quicksand, as you don't want to get sucked under!

RAINBOW QUICKSAND

1. Take the objects that you or your kids have collected and sort them into a few colour categories as closely as possible.

2. Scatter them casually over the floor in an open space – we always do this in our living room – and tell your kids to get jumping about. I tend to let mine jump on our sofa to stay off the floor, but that's up to you.

3. If you are organized, you could label some lolly sticks with the colours on them to pull out at random, or you can simply call out a colour. Your kids then have to dash and stand on that coloured object.

MUSICAL QUICKSAND

1. This is a twist on musical chairs as you'll be removing a stepping stone each time you turn the music off, which makes the game harder as you go on.

2. Stick on some upbeat music that you all enjoy listening to (we opt for a party music playlist) and tell them to dance around whilst making sure they keep to the stepping stones.

3. Stop the music, and make sure everyone is off the ground. Remove one stepping stone and continue playing.

4. Keep removing a stepping stone each time, making it harder to stay out of the quicksand.

5. The person who hasn't fallen into the quicksand by the end or the last person standing is the winner.

TOP TIP: Save coloured paper in a plastic wallet and stash somewhere near the TV. You can whip it out easily and get playing immediately.

QUICK OFF THE MARK TIC-TAC-TOE

Tic-tac-toe is another name for noughts and crosses, a game that has been popular since Roman times! This classic challenge is played on a grid of three squares by three squares, and the aim is to get either three noughts or crosses in a row, taking it in turns to play. Whilst you can play it with pens and paper, this version turns it into a race, where players run to one of nine markers on the floor (ideas below) and drop their counters (noughts and crosses), which can be played indoors or outside and will add some real excitement to the rainiest of Sunday afternoons.

TOP TIP: Collect twelve rocks when you are next out and about. Wash and paint them, half one colour or design and half another. Use them as counters for your tic-tac-toe game – it is great practice and knowing the possible formations will make the physical game more competitive!

WHAT YOU NEED

THE GRID

You need nine markers to put on the floor to act as your board. These could be hula hoops, plastic or paper plates, pieces of paper stuck down with masking tape – it really doesn't matter what you use so long as you can clearly mark out three rows of three.

THE COUNTERS

Each team or person needs six items that are the same colour to drop onto the board on the floor. Bean bags, Lego pieces, plastic bowls, coloured scarves, tea towels, painted rocks, whatever you have!

HOW IT WORKS

1. Ask your kids to help you to decide where best to lay the grid on the floor. You want this to be a few metres away from where you will be standing to start as the aim is to run up to the board to play, and then return and tag a partner to go next.

2. Lay out your grid markers on the floor, evenly spaced, so that there are three rows of three. If you're sticking paper down, it is best to do this now.

3. Decide on your starting line and pop something down on the floor so that it is clear and helps to make the game fair.

4. If there are two players, what you will do next is race from the start line to the grid and drop your marker down in a place on the grid, and race back to the start line. You then repeat this strategy each time until there is a winner. The quicker you get to the board, the more likely the chances of winning as you can choose where your marker goes.

5. If you are playing in a group of four or more, it's really fun to play this as a relay race. When you start, the first person for each team runs up and places their marker down before racing back and tagging the next person, making sure they cross the start line when they return. The partner then runs up and places a marker and so on. You keep going in this relay formation until there is a winner!

SPIN-THE-BOTTLE TWISTER

I absolutely love this game – always have and always will. It's so great when a game transcends time, fads and fashions. And this is definitely one of those games. Twister is a physical challenge where a referee spins a wheel and calls out a limb and a colour and the people playing have to match up their body part with a coloured circle on the mat. It usually involves a grid of twenty-four circles where each row of six circles is a different colour. One thing I've found is that the shop-bought version of this game is too big for my kids to play. But by making your own, you can tailor it to suit your smaller people.

TOP TIP: Set up a 'junk bin' at home where you put bits of recycling that look like they may come in handy in the future, such as small drinks bottles and paper plates. I'm always fishing in mine for things to use.

WHAT YOU NEED

- A paper plate
- Small empty plastic drinks bottle
- Fabric to make a playing surface: an old bedsheet, shower curtain or tablecloth
- Four colours of paint, or permanent pens such as Sharpies

HOW IT WORKS

1. Make your playing mat by taking your fabric and marking it up with four rows of six circles. Using a kids' plastic bowl as a template works well. Normally these are spaced apart, but small people might benefit from a smaller board. Get your kids to stretch out on the floor to see what will work best for you.

2. Paint onto your fabric with four colours of paint so that each row of six circles is a different colour, or simply mark the outline of each circle with a marker pen to show which is which.

3. Now take your paper plate and draw a cross on it to divide it into four sections. Then write a label on each of the four sections: left hand, right hand, left foot, right foot. For each section, mark four coloured circles on the rim of the plate, so that each limb can go to any of the four colours. You are now ready to play!

4. Lay your playing mat on the ground and ask all players to remove their shoes before you begin. Each player must then place their feet on the closest yellow and blue circles.

5. The referee spins the empty bottle on the plate and reads out the limb and colour that the bottle lands closest to. Only one limb per player per circle, and if there is a dispute, the referee must decide who got there first.

6. Keep spinning the bottle and changing the moves. The first person to end up on the floor is out and the last one still off the floor is the winner.

ICE (MOP THE FLOOR) HOCKEY

What if I told you that by doing this activity your kids will clean the floor in the process? Pretty appealing, right? I can't guarantee they'll do a good job, but from where I'm standing, every little helps. By freezing discs of ice in small plastic bowls the night before, you'll have real ice pucks to play with, which adds fun and speed to the game, as you need to play before they melt! If you'd rather not get your floors wet, this is also a great game to play outside; the smoother the playing surface, the better.

TOP TIP: Make a stock of ice pucks in advance. Fill as many small plastic bowls one third full with water as your freezer can handle. Pop them in overnight, and when they have hardened, run warm water over the bowls to remove them. Stick them in freezer bags or wrap them in cling film and you'll have a stock of pucks in your freezer ready to play at any time.

WHAT YOU NEED
- Ice pucks (made the night before; see above)
- 2 mops or brooms – full size or children's toy ones
- 2 buckets for goals

HOW IT WORKS
1. This is a game for two players, who will each be equipped with a mop and must defend their goal (bucket) from the puck that comes their way.

2. Define the playing area for the game and how much space you want to have between each goal, which may depend on the age of your kids. You might like to use masking tape to mark the perimeter of the playing zone, or you can just let them get on with it.

3. Each person playing needs a mop or broom. We have a toy cleaning station with a mop and broom, so my kids use that. Older kids should be fine with an ordinary-sized mop, and for the record, any mop will do. If you have hockey or croquet sticks, you can also play with those.

4. Now it is time to play! The aim is to get the puck into the other person's goal as many times as you can before it is bashed to pieces or simply melts. It is useful for someone to keep score of the goals so that there is a clear winner at the end.

5. You can then surprise your kids with their reward for taking part in the game, which is to clean the floor they have just played on! Good luck!

HANDS AND FEET LADDER HOP

This game is one for all the family and has had us in stitches just trying to do the moves. It involves placing your hands and feet on paper marked with either foot- or handprints in the shape of a ladder. For each rung of the ladder, there are three pieces of paper with two feet and one hand, or two hands and one foot, in a different pattern each time. Trying to hop and place your hands and feet on the right card is both challenging and hilarious, whilst also being great for coordination. Making the cards up is an easy art activity and so, all in all, that's your afternoon inside sorted.

TOP TIP: If you are playing this with adults, use A4 paper. If you are playing with smaller children, cut the paper in half to make A5 so that it's more manageable. And if you have a laminating machine, you can make your resources last by laminating them before first use.

WHAT YOU NEED

- Plain paper (at least 18 sheets)
- Masking tape or Blu-Tack
- Washable paint or felt-tip pens

HOW IT WORKS

1. Imagine a ladder with six rungs. On each rung, imagine three cards. On each of these cards, imagine either a foot or handprint. This is the template for the game. All you need to do is make the cards and you're good to go.

2. Now, you want to make nine footprints and nine handprints on separate pieces of paper. There are two ways of doing this. You can either draw around your kids' or your own hands and feet nine times on separate pieces of paper with a felt tip, or paint your hands and feet with washable paint and print them onto the paper. This is messier – and you'll need to do it well in advance so that they dry in time – but the shapes are clearer.

3. Choose a nice open space to play in and arrange your eighteen pieces of paper on the floor in a ladder shape, with three cards per rung. Make sure you only have two hand or footprints per rung and that they're all pointing in the same direction, away from where you will start. Mix up the order so that each rung of the ladder has a different sequence of hand and footprints.

4. Stick down the prints using either Blu-Tack or masking tape. You want them to be fairly securely attached, as they will be trodden and jumped on.

5. Now let the games commence! Take it in turns to see if you can jump up the ladder, placing your hands and feet on the right card each time. You will always have one foot or hand spare, and so there is a bit of balancing involved. If you fall over or get it wrong, you have to go back to the start and join the end of the queue.

1. Escape Room with Clues

2. Blindfold Sensory Challenge

3. Googly Eyes Photo Challenge

4. Instant Jigsaws

5. Toothpick Towers

6. Ultimate Spiral Marble Run

7. Lolly Stick Games

8. Toy Zip Wire

9. Family and Friends Guess Who

10. Frozen Palace Messy Play

SCREEN-FREE GAME TIME

This is the chapter to flick to when you've run out of things to do, you've had enough of the same old toys on the shelf and you know deep down you have it in you to create some fun, but just need a nudge. Well, consider this your nudge! And don't get me wrong, I'm not saying screen time is bad. Far from it. In fact, I don't know how I would have survived parenthood without it. It just seems like a good idea to have a few more tricks up your sleeve. The activities in this chapter are an eclectic mix essentially designed to help you fill the hours, minutes and seconds until bedtime. There are challenges, games and all sorts of screen-free fun, mainly for your kids but also for you – you might surprise yourself and enjoy making an ice palace or marble run more than you think.

ESCAPE ROOM WITH CLUES

Escape rooms have been incredibly popular in recent years and it is easy to understand why. The basic premise of solving a set of problems or cracking a series of codes in a given time frame is thrilling, encourages team work and gets the cogs whirring in your brain without it feeling like 'work' (or perhaps 'school'). It is called an escape room on the basis that you cannot leave the room until the challenges are complete. Essentially, so long as you set a series of challenges for your kids to do in a sequence, you'll have an escape room.

Here are ten (yes, ten!) challenges you could incorporate into your escape room to keep your kids occupied and out of mischief. And if they're a little bit older, why not challenge them to create their own escape room?

TOP TIP: Theme your escape room, simply by playing some music in the background or getting your kids to dress up. From Harry Potter to escaping Rapunzel's tower, there is a lot to choose from!

THE AIM:

Your kids have to solve clues that give them a piece of information each time. That information adds up to some sort of answer, which will then free them from the escape room or win them a prize. My preference is that each challenge reveals a letter, which together make up a word that is the password to a treat, awarded by a grown-up (who hopefully during the game can enjoy a cuppa and put their feet up!).

1. FALSE BOTTOM BOX: Take a normal delivery box and cut out a piece of card so that it sits flat inside the box. Put your clue inside the base of the box and lay the false bottom on top. Pop the box somewhere not too obvious and tell your kids their first clue is 'boxed up'.

2. X MARKS THE SPOT: Draw a rough diagram of the room in which you are going to hide your clue and add an X to mark where you are going to hide it. Now hide the clue, but make it extremely hard to find (I've taped clues under my sofa before).

3. PADLOCKED SCISSORS: Write your clue on a piece of paper, fold it up and place it inside a box or old food packaging and seal shut with sticky tape. Now take a pair of scissors and pop a padlock through its handles. Tell your kids that a memorable date will unlock the padlock (check it is set for a family birthday or similar) and when they've managed this, they can use the scissors to cut up the package and reveal the clue.

4. FREEZER FUN: This is one of my favourites! Write your clue in permanent marker on a piece of paper and fold it up or scrunch it into a ball. Pop in a plastic food container and fill three quarters full with water. Freeze until solid. The challenge is to crack open the ice to reveal what is on the paper.

5. ALL RIPPED UP: This is perhaps the simplest of them all. Take a piece of newspaper and write the clue on it relatively small amid the text. Now tear up the paper (not too small) and place the bits in an envelope or bag for kids to find and piece back together.

6. FOOTPRINT MATCH UP: Take a shoe with a clear pattern on the sole and paint the sole with washable paint. Print the sole of the shoe on paper to make a footprint. Clean the sole of the shoe, pop the clue inside the shoe and return it to where it belongs. Your kids have to match the footprint with the shoe to find the clue.

7. MORSE CODE: Write out your clue in Morse code and then give your kids a copy of the code itself (you can easily find it online). They then have to match up the symbols with what you have written to reveal the answer.

8. BOOKISH: Write your clue on a piece of paper and hide it inside a book on a bookcase or shelf. That's it. Your kids will have to flick, sift and sort through the pages of the books to find the paper, but they can't pass the challenge unless all the books are back where they belong at the end.

9. EXTRA JIGSAW: Take a jigsaw in a box and add in one extra piece from another puzzle of a similar type. On the back of the piece you added in, write your clue faintly in pencil. Tell your kids that by putting the puzzle together the clue will be revealed, and leave it at that!

10. ELASTIC BAND BALL: This is definitely a 'make the night before' activity! Write your clue on paper and scrunch it up into a ball. Wrap elastic bands and/or hairbands around it so that you get a ball of bands, however big you want. You kids will have to unwrap the bands to reveal the clue – you might want to give them a set time in which they have to do it.

BLINDFOLD SENSORY CHALLENGE

I can still recall a blindfolded food tasting activity from my childhood where I bit into a raw potato to guess what it was. I'm not sure what the aim was there, but I certainly didn't enjoy it! This activity is totally different. You aren't trying to trick your kids into eating things they don't like, but encouraging them to be adventurous and explore new tastes, flavours, textures and smells in the form of a game, so even the most cautious children should be willing to give it a go. This activity is split up into three parts and you can opt to do just one part of it, or all three.

TASTE CHALLENGE

WHAT YOU NEED

- Foods for tasting: This is a personal choice and you should take into account any allergies and what your kids are likely to have fun tasting. Fruit and vegetables work brilliantly. In addition, we have tried out the following: cubes of pickled cucumber, dark chocolate chips, grated cheese, spoons of jelly, salt and vinegar crisps, baked beans, slices of boiled egg, snippets of smoked salmon and spoons of ice cream.

- A plate for each player

- Cups of water

- Scarf, tie or blindfold for each player

HOW IT WORKS

1. Prepare a different plate of small items of food for each child. If you have more than one child playing and they see what each other has to try, it will be easy to guess when it's their turn. Cover the plates with foil until you're ready to start.

2. Explain to your kids that the best chefs in the world have had to sample all sorts of food to know what tastes good and which flavours go well together. And today they are going to be chefs in training! Tell them that the aim of the game is to identify different foods and see which taste good together, and that you haven't included anything that you know they really don't like.

3. Blindfold your kids, taking it in turns as necessary, and let them taste the food on the plate you have prepared. Keep a tally if you like of how many they get correct.

SMELL CHALLENGE

WHAT YOU NEED

- Different items that have a distinctive smell, such as: rosemary, lavender, apples, strawberries, cheese, bread, fruit juice, garlic, onion, ginger, pencil shavings, cloves, ground coffee, vanilla essence, mint.
- A small bowl for each item
- A scarf, tie or blindfold for each player

HOW IT WORKS

1. Put a small amount of each item in a small bowl so that your kids can smell but not touch the item. As with the taste challenge, you might want to have different items for each child so they won't already know what they are when it is their turn.

2. Blindfold the player taking part and ask them to hold each bowl in turn and take a good long sniff to see if they can work out what the item is. It is fun to write down their answers and keep a tally of who is correct.

3. Repeat this step for each player and when you have all had a go, add up how many each person got right.

TOUCH CHALLENGE

WHAT YOU NEED

- For the sensory challenge: different items that have a distinctive feel or texture such as sand, feathers, cotton wool, leaves, beads, bubbles or foam, polystyrene, wet sponges
- For the items challenge: household objects or toys and a bag or pillowcase to hold them in
- A scarf, tie or blindfold for each player

HOW IT WORKS

1. If you are using sensory items such as sand and feathers, prepare a small amount of each in a suitable container and lay them out on a flat surface. If you have more than one child playing, pick a few for each player to guess.

2. A simpler option is to fill a bag or sack with a variety of different toys and household items that can be pulled out and guessed. You can choose any items that are easy to handle and distinctive to feel: kitchen utensils, soft toys, Lego and jigsaw pieces, socks, rubber balls, even the TV remote control.

3. Decide on how many items each player has to guess and then blindfold them and let them see if they can work out what each item is by touching the item in the dish or pulling an item out of the bag.

4. Keep a tally of how many correct answers each player gets and add them up at the end.

GOOGLY EYES PHOTO CHALLENGE

Here's a word I didn't know existed until recently. The word is pareidolia and it is used to describe the tendency to see recognizable shapes or patterns in ordinary things. So, for example, seeing shapes in clouds, faces or figures in nature, even an image on a bit of burnt toast. This activity encourages you and your kids to do just this – look for images hidden in ordinary items – and then turn it into a photo challenge. You only need a smartphone, a packet of stick-on googly eyes, some time and your imagination. This is quick, simple fun and can be done indoors or out. It's perfect to fall back on when you feel you've run out of inspiration and need something quick.

TOP TIP: Remember the craze for 'eyebombing'? This is the art of sticking googly eyes on ordinary objects in public spaces to spread a bit of cheer. Whilst I don't recommend doing this specifically, checking it out online will give your kids some great inspiration for their own googly eye challenge.

WHAT YOU NEED

- A smartphone or camera
- Googly eye stickers – the sort that have an adhesive back and black dots that move around inside a clear plastic top

HOW IT WORKS

1. Explain to your kids that you're going to be finding faces that are hidden around the house, on a walk or in the garden, and that these faces are missing their eyes. It is their job to find the faces and give them eyes.

2. Give your kids an example of how this could work. Find an object or part of your home nearby and stick on two googly eyes to show how adding eyes to the right thing can create a face.

3. If your kids are old enough, send them off with a few googly eyes (they can be reused each time as you won't be leaving the stickers in situ) and a smartphone or camera, and tell them to find as many faces as they can in a given time frame. Depending on the age of your kids, you might want to put the smartphone on airplane mode and turn the Wi-Fi off.

4. If your kids are a bit younger, go around your home or an outside space with them and help them to see where there might be a face, and then let them stick the eyes on and take a photo.

ONE STEP FURTHER

Print out the pictures of the results of your googly eyes in situ (I'd suggest nine small pictures per A4 piece of paper) and then let your kids give each face a name. They could cut them out and use them in art, for a collage or even create a comic strip with their new characters.

INSTANT JIGSAWS

This one is a fun one. Fun for the kids, but also fun for the grown-ups. And there is no prep because your kids are going to help you set up. Essentially, all you need to do is cut up pictures and packaging into random shapes, and in doing so turn them into instant jigsaws. Whilst it may sound like one of the simplest activities out there, there are lots of hidden benefits to doing jigsaws, which is why I was so keen to include it. Every time your kids do jigsaws, they are exercising their brains. Jigsaws use both the left and right side of the brain, can help to improve short-term memory and boost spatial awareness, and are great for stress relief.

TOP TIP: Label zip-lock bags with permanent pens or labels if you have them to describe the jigsaw inside each one. It is also worth collecting colourful boxes and magazines in advance, so you have a stack to play with.

WHAT YOU NEED

- Cardboard packaging such as chocolate boxes or cereal boxes
- Printed photographs or ordinary photographs that are spare
- Zip-lock or freezer bags
- Scissors

HOW IT WORKS

1. Lay out all of your packaging and photographs on a table, together with the scissors and zip-lock bags.

2. If you would like to make photograph jigsaws, stick photographs down onto your cardboard packaging. Otherwise, the pattern on your cardboard will be the jigsaw image to piece together.

3. Give everyone a pen or pencil and tell them to draw some straight lines, some zigzag lines and a few squiggly shapes on the reverse side of the cardboard.

4. Now cut out the cardboard along some of the lines – there's no need to follow them exactly; they are there as a guide and to help children visualize where to cut.

5. Keep the pieces in a pile and when all the cutting is done, put the pieces into a zip-lock or freezer bag.

6. You can now swap bags with your family members and repeat as many times as you like. The smaller the pieces, the harder it is to put together!

TOOTHPICK TOWERS

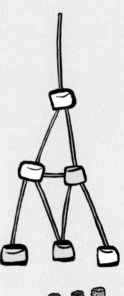

I'm fairly certain that if you tell your kids that you've got an activity planned that involves a pile of sweets, they're going to be pretty up for the task. And if you'd prefer not to use sweets, the challenge to see who can build the tallest tower is still going to sound pretty exciting.

There is no prep for this game – all you do is lay out toothpicks (or spaghetti) and 'cement', and let the building commence. At the same time you'll be promoting STEM learning and encouraging your kids to think about important questions such as how do buildings stay up? What stops them from falling over? And how do they get to be so high? I hope you enjoy building your gravity-defying towers as much as we did!

TOP TIP: Take photos of local buildings when you're out and about and also of your home from the outside. The familiarity of buildings kids recognize will encourage them to take part in the activity.

WHAT YOU NEED

- A pack of toothpicks per person, or use dried spaghetti
- A packet of fruit pastilles or some mini marshmallows; or for a sugar-free version, use Blu-Tack or play dough
- Optional but helpful: pictures of buildings

HOW IT WORKS

1. You need a big flat surface for this to work – a kitchen or dining table is ideal. Mark out a building station for each kid with a tray or chopping board. This will let you move your buildings around if you need to. Lay out your toothpicks or spaghetti and your chosen form of 'cement', along with any pictures of buildings you have.

2. Explain to your kids that this is a family challenge to see who can build the tallest tower that stays up, using only toothpicks and sweets or Blu-Tack/play dough. Or you may prefer to ask your kids to build the most interesting towers they can, providing they stay up.

3. If you're using dried spaghetti instead of toothpicks, it is helpful to snap them into pieces of equal size. Smaller children may like to help you do this. Spaghetti may be preferable for smaller hands as toothpicks are quite pointy. Choose whatever you think will work best with your kids.

4. Now let them start to explore how to build with the resources you have laid out. They'll need to think about the base of their tower, how to make it strong, and how to ensure it doesn't topple over!

5. You may like to have prizes ready at the end. However, we have found that eating some of the fruit pastilles (our preferred cement) is reward enough.

ULTIMATE SPIRAL MARBLE RUN

My two-year-old loves to scribble in a circle, over and over again, and it is quite mesmerizing to watch, until, of course, she throws the pens on the floor and scrunches up the paper. That aside, there really is something beautiful about circles and spirals and this activity demonstrates that. By creating a spiral using paper plates stuck to a tube, you can make a marble run which can lead to some really relaxing play. Making the marble run is a simple craft activity and great time filler, and it uses items I suspect you'll have at home. I suggest starting with eight paper plates, but as you'll be building your marble run structure upwards, you can add as many as you like.

TOP TIP: If you are able to use different coloured paper plates, your marble run will resemble a rainbow. Similarly, painting your kitchen roll or loo roll tubes beforehand can make this look even more fantastic.

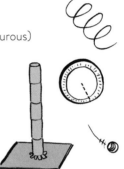

WHAT YOU NEED

- 8 paper plates (more if you're feeling adventurous)
- 2 kitchen roll tubes or 5 toilet roll tubes
- 1 roughly A4-sized piece of card (delivery box cardboard is ideal)
- Some marbles or small rubber balls
- Sticky tape
- A glue gun
- Newspaper
- A small plastic bowl or dish

NOTE: Marbles and small balls are dangerous if swallowed and so please keep them out of the reach of children under three and make sure children are supervised.

HOW IT WORKS

1. Place one of your kitchen or loo roll tubes upright on a paper plate and draw around the end. Cut this out with scissors and then use it as a template for the other paper plates. All your eight (or more) paper plates should have a hole in the middle.

2. Now make one cut in each paper plate, from the edge to the circle in the centre, so that you can lift one side up and one side down.

3. You want your pole in the middle of the marble run to be around 35cm high, so tape together your tubes to make them the right length. Scrunch up some newspaper and poke it down the middle of your pole to make it as strong as possible.

4. Make a series of 1cm-long snips around one end of the pole, so that you can splay them out and later stick them down to the cardboard base to keep the marble run secure.

5. Now take a pencil and make a mark 3cm above the snips you have just made. This is where the end of your first plate will be stuck. Go up the pole, making a mark every 3cm until you've done this eight times (or as many times as you have plates).

6. Take your first plate and apply some glue from your glue gun around the middle circle. Now stick it around your pole, so that one end meets the first line you've drawn and then wrap it around so that the other end meets the next line, 3cm up.

7. Do the same with your next plate, lining up the edge of the first one with the second. When you've stuck it to the pole and it is secure, pop some sticky tape between the two plate edges to make a smooth run for the marble to go down.

8. Repeat this step for the remaining plates, so that they spiral up the pole and are attached to each other with sticky tape each time.

9. When your marble run is complete, apply some glue to the snipped flaps at the base of the pole, splay them out and stick them down to the cardboard base.

10. Pop a bowl at the end of your marble run to catch them as they fly down and you are ready to experiment with your new toy creation.

LOLLY STICK GAMES

The humble lolly stick is not to be underestimated. If you've only ever come into contact with a lolly stick when you've finished your chocolate Feast (is there a better lolly out there? It's basically a chocolate bar on a stick!), let me be the first to tell you there is a whole world of super fun and super quick games you can try. By writing words on lolly sticks, you can create a storytelling game. By marking lolly sticks with patterns and shapes using a felt tip, you can whip up a memory game in minutes. Plus, they are great for making quick ice lollies – just stick them into a small pot of yoghurt or fromage frais (yes, through the lid), leave them in the freezer until solid, and voilà, a 'home-made' ice lolly, good to go.

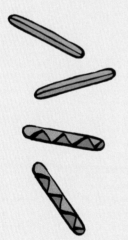

TOP TIP: Give your kids some lolly sticks and ask them to come up with a list of all the possible uses for a lolly stick, from an oar for a mouse to a toothpick for a giant. Encourage those imaginations to run wild and free.

WHAT YOU NEED
- A pack of lolly sticks (I'd buy a pack of 100 to begin with)
- Felt-tip pens

HOW IT WORKS
I couldn't decide which game to include, so here are both.

LOLLY STICK STORY GAME
1. Get your kids to write down nouns (objects) on some of your lolly sticks, or have them tell you objects for you to write down for them. Aim for more than ten (and as many as you like).

2. Put them inside a bag or box and then use them as stimuli to tell stories. For example, you could ask everyone to pull out three lolly sticks and make up a story with them. Or you could tell a story by pulling lolly sticks out as you go. Or even take it in turns to tell the next line of a story that has to involve a lolly stick from the bag.

3. You could theme your lolly sticks and group them together, for example nouns to do with the seaside, a favourite family film or types of food.

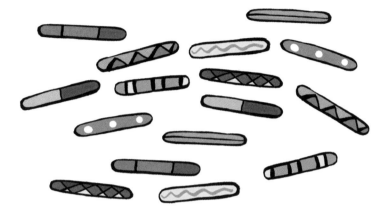

LOLLY STICK SNAP

1. Grab some felt tips and forty lolly sticks and line them up in pairs on a flat surface. Explain to your kids that they can help you mark the sticks and that pairs of sticks have to be identical (or near enough).

2. On each pair of lolly sticks, draw a pattern such as dots in a colour sequence, zigzag lines, letters, shapes and so on. So long as the reverse side is left totally clear, it doesn't matter what you do, so long as they match up, and so toddler scribbles are great too!

3. When finished, mix all your lolly sticks up and lay them face down on a flat surface so that you can't see the patterns underneath.

4. You are ready to play snap. Each player picks up a stick to start with and you take it in turns to turn over a lolly stick each time, trying to match them up with the one in your hand.

TOY ZIP WIRE

Whenever we go to the park, and there is a zip wire, my kids make a run for it. And in all honesty, when I was a kid, I was obsessed with zip wires too. That feeling of freedom that comes from whizzing through the breeze is magical. Saying that, I'm a bit afraid of heights and so anything too high up and I think I'll pass! What's fun about making a toy zip wire at home is that it brings your kids' toys to life – teddy bears and dolls are suddenly able to move! And this activity has been kept as simple as possible so that you can just set up and go.

TOP TIP: If you want to encourage a bit of learning alongside the fun, talk to your kids about what might slow the toys down and what might speed them up when they go down the zip wire. You could also ask them about why different kinds of surfaces might work better or worse for a zip wire.

WHAT YOU NEED

- A ball of string, twine or some plastic-coated wire
- A clothes hanger – ideally a small children's one
- A variety of different toys
- Washing pegs
- Sticky tape
- Pipe cleaners

HOW IT WORKS

1. The first decision is where your zip wire is going to be positioned. You'll need to have a bit of space and a descent so that the toys get some momentum as they fly down! I would suggest down a flight of stairs, over a banister or even out of a window into your outside space. Everyone's home is different, and so pick a space and size that will work for you.

2. Take your string and attach it at the top and bottom to something secure such as a banister or door handle (providing the door is shut) in the area you have selected. How long you make your zip wire is up to you!

3. Take some toys and attach them in turn to your clothes hanger, or to multiple hangers if you have spares. Use pipe cleaners or pegs to do this, depending on the size of your toys, how big and how heavy they are. Getting your kids to work out how best to attach the toys to the hanger is great for their problem-solving skills, so don't do the hard work for them!

4. Now simply have fun hooking the toys at the top of the zip line and seeing how fast they travel to the bottom! It is great to time each toy and have a conversation about why some might go faster than others. And have your phone or camera ready – toys hurtling down a zip wire really do make a great picture or video!

FAMILY AND FRIENDS GUESS WHO

I'm borrowing a bit of my history teaching experience for this activity as I have previously made Guess Who games to help students remember who was who in the past, and it really is so fun! Guess Who is a game played between two people who have identical boards with a set of faces on them. You take it in turns to pick a card from a pack with the same set of faces as the boards, and your opponent asks questions to work out which card you have got by eliminating characters on their board.

WHAT YOU NEED

- Three A4-sized pieces of cardboard – slightly thicker than a cereal box would be ideal
- Small printouts of the faces of family and friends (they should all fit onto one sheet of A4 paper when printed)
- A glue stick
- Sharp scissors or a craft knife

TOP TIP: Ask your friends and family to send you a picture in advance that they are happy for you to use. This way, you can play it with them if they ever pop round!

HOW IT WORKS

1. The first thing you need to do is collect photos of family and friends that you can use. Copy them into a Word document so that they all fit on the page. Five rows of four photos work well so that you have twenty photos in total.

2. Print off this document three times. You will need one copy for each board and one to create the set of cards to pick from.

3. Take one of your A4-sized pieces of card and stick down one of your printouts. Now using sharp scissors or a craft knife, cut out each of the pictures. These will be your pack of cards.

4. Next, you need to make the two boards using the two remaining pieces of card. Draw twenty rectangles onto the card, the same size roughly as your printed pictures. Now cut along the three sides of each rectangle closest to you, so that each rectangle is now like a flap that can be lifted up. I would hand over the drawing and measuring up to any kids that are old enough to help you with this as it's a good way to practise a bit of maths!

5. Cut up the photographs and stick them down, one on each flap on your two boards. It doesn't matter which order they are in and the boards will ideally be different in terms of layout.

6. You should now have two boards and a pack of cards with a photo of each of the people involved in your game, and so the fun bit can commence! One player picks a card and conceals it from the other player, who has to ask a set number of questions to see if they can work out who it is.

7. The reason this is SO fun is because you don't have to just describe the person's appearance. You can ask questions about things you know about them, for example, 'Does the person on your card drive a blue car?'

FROZEN PALACE MESSY PLAY

Messy play is essential. Messy play is learning. Messy play helps kids to connect with the world around them. Messy play supports communication, particularly before words are spoken or when they are perhaps tricky to say. Messy play promotes physical development and it also fosters independent learning in kids of all ages. There are, therefore, very few reasons not to give it a go. But, and I know what you are going to say, what about the mess? Well, let me present to you frozen palace messy play, where you're literally building a palace from ice, so the only risk is getting a bit wet. Yes, I've included shaving foam and some paint, but stay with me. This activity can occupy kids for hours – and on that basis, it's worth giving it a go.

WHAT YOU NEED
- Plastic cups, bowls, food containers and other freezer-safe moulds
- A large tray, plastic box or Tuff Tray
- A large bowl
- Shaving foam
- Washable paint
- Paintbrushes

TOP TIP: Ask your kids to describe to you their ultimate palace or get them to draw a picture. What shape is the roof? Is it one big structure or lots of little ones? Are there any special features such as a bridge, moat or turrets? This will get them excited and thinking about what they can build.

HOW IT WORKS

1. The night before: clear a space in your freezer and fill as many plastic bowls, cups, silicone cupcake cases, jelly moulds, food boxes and other small and freezer friendly containers with water. Put them in the freezer and leave to harden overnight.

2. Explain to your kids that they are going to build the palace of their dreams, out of ice! Decide on a good space to do this (outside would be ideal) and lay out the plastic tray or box that you are going to use to build on. The ice will melt and so bear this in mind.

3. Take the containers out of the freezer and let your kids help you get the ice out of each one. Place the pieces on the tray along with some metal spoons which can be used for chipping at the ice.

4. Squirt out the shaving foam into a large bowl and pop in a few spoons for your kids to use. This can be cement, snow, sea, mountains . . .

5. Water down a few colours of washable paint by adding about a teaspoon of water to each tablespoon of paint (although don't feel you have to measure, you just want a runnier consistency) and put these into small plastic bowls along with a paintbrush. The ice will clean the paintbrushes and so no need for a separate bowl of water.

6. Now sit back and let your kids chip, paint, mould, lift, manoeuvre and create their palace out of ice – and don't forget to take a photo of the finished product at the end.

1. Magical Fairy Garden

2. Mud on the Menu

3. Nature Picture Frames

4. Bottle Bee Hotel

5. Hubble Bubble Magic Potions

6. Butterfly Wings Three Ways

7. Terrarium Mini Garden

8. Coffee Rock Treasure Eggs

9. Dandelion Honey

10. Fat Cake Bird Feeder

THE GREAT OUTDOORS

Going outside is good for us. Fact. However, never have the benefits of the great outdoors been more challenged by the lure of technology than today. And there is no escaping the fact that today's children spend less time outside than the generation before them. Anything we can do with our kids to get them outside and engaging with nature is worthwhile. Not only are the health and wellbeing benefits huge, but using nature as a source of play and inspiration is largely cost-free. A big bonus for me is that any mess created outside can usually stay there. The activities in this chapter aim to busy your kids outside in a variety of fun, interesting and imaginative ways that will foster their creativity. I hope you enjoy doing them as much as we have.

MAGICAL FAIRY GARDEN

Right at the beginning of the coronavirus lockdown, my five-year-old daughter told me that she wanted to build a fairy garden, and in her words, 'right now, Mummy'. I panicked. What were we going to use? I'd never made one before and my usual trick of planning things in advance was useless. My reply, because why not, was 'yes, of course', whilst I fumbled around the house for ideas. Meanwhile, she had gone outside and had started to make a pile of nature from our garden to use. It was one of those moments where you're reminded that sometimes all you actually need are the things right in front of you. The beauty of a fairy garden here is that anything goes – and for me, not being prepared made it work even better.

WHAT YOU NEED

- A container: bucket, plant pot, barrel, trough, planter or large tin
- Soil (any) or sand (any) for the base
- Greenery to cover the soil, such as moss or grass
- Small stones, rocks, pebbles, marbles, beads or buttons
- Twigs, sticks, bark, wood chips, small logs
- Miniature toys: small figures, Lego
- Optional items to make it sparkle: foil, biodegradable glitter, old CDs

TOP TIP: Get your kids to draw their fairy garden beforehand if they are able to, and set a timer for a couple of minutes for them to go on a 'fairy house hunt' around your home to find things they could use.

HOW IT WORKS

1. Your container will be the base for your fairy garden and everything that you use will go inside it. I recommend using a container as it makes moving your fairy garden around easy to do and means you can make it indoors if the weather isn't so great.

2. Fill your fairy garden container with soil or sand up to your desired level. If your container is quite big, it might be better to fill it half full, whereas for a small plant pot, filling it to the top might work better.

3. Every fairy garden needs a dwelling of some sort to keep the fairies safe from harm! You may already have a toy you can use for this, but if not, we have used twigs and leaves to create a fairy teepee and also a really small broken plant pot, which we turned upside down in the soil. You can paint and decorate the dwelling you make with any craft items you have or leave it natural – no one size fits all.

4. Now it is time to consider the garden itself and this is the really fun bit, where your kids' imaginations can run wild! We rolled up foil to make little silver balls, collected small stones to make a path and found fallen leaves still on their branches, which we stuck into the soil to act as trees.

5. While you are making and decorating your garden, chat to your kids about what they want and how they're going to make it happen. This activity is a wonderful way of not only engaging your kids in nature but also encouraging them to articulate their thoughts. The open-endedness of making a fairy garden will hopefully inspire them to see their surroundings in a different way and encourage them to think about the ways in which we can use nature around us for play.

MUD ON
THE MENU

This activity takes zero prep, and all you need are ordinary kitchen resources and an outside space, whether at home or out and about. By asking your kids to turn mud and the nature around it into food (not to be eaten, I should add) with some good suggestions and structured advice, you can unlock a world of imaginary play with whatever your outdoor surroundings have to offer. And, very importantly, it might give you some much-needed peace and quiet! I've selected three simple ideas here that you can try. If it doesn't float your kids' boat, at least there was no investment on your part, and hopefully the mess is outside, so no clearing up!

WHAT YOU NEED

This really can be a resource-free activity; however, the following make it extra fun and allow more structured play:

- Kitchen utensils made of plastic, metal or silicone
- Cupcake or muffin cases
- Cupcake or muffin baking tray
- Cake tins or paper tin liners
- Mixing bowls, measuring cups and plastic jugs, it's great to keep a bag of old or spare kitchen items that you don't mind being used outside handy in a small bag or box for easy play time

HOW IT WORKS

1. They key to this activity is the set-up. Explain to your kids that they're going to be using the great outdoors to make imaginary food and that they can let their imagination run wild. If your kids are a bit older, they might like to come up with a menu or even a name for an imaginary restaurant.

2. Some kids are not so keen on getting their hands dirty, and if this applies to your family, they can still play along with gloves on, using utensils or focusing on decoration.

3. Decide on the space you're going to use. If you have more than one participant, perhaps let them mark out their own areas.

4. Now it's time to get busy. To help you along, here are three suggestions on what your kids could focus on:

MUD PIES: In a cake or pie dish, pat down some mud as if it is pastry, then add any fillings such as leaves or grass, before topping with another layer of mud and patting it down. You could even try taking a slice and seeing if it holds its shape.

NATURE CUPCAKES: Fill a cupcake or muffin baking tray with cupcake cases if you have them, or leave it bare if not. Let your kids fill each hole with mud to act as the sponge and then decorate with leaves, petals, stones or anything else around you.

FLOWER SOUP: Fill a mixing bowl half full with water and then let your kids add in bits of nature as they like. It is best not to add mud to this one if you want your soup to remain relatively clear.

NOTE: Little hands will need a good scrub with an antibacterial soap when they have finished this activity. Equally, any kitchen utensils should be thoroughly cleaned and sterilized before being used for food preparation.

NATURE PICTURE FRAMES

If you have any cardboard and some scissors, then this next activity is one to try. By simply cutting different-shaped holes in cardboard and using different forms of nature to fill in the gap, you'll be amazed at the results. If you have any of the *That's not my . . .* books lurking around, you'll notice it is the same principle.

WHAT YOU NEED

- Cardboard from a cereal or delivery box
- Sharp scissors
- Pen or pencil

TOP TIP: Print out photos of family or friends to use for your nature frames. Sticking down the head from a photo, and then drawing and cutting out the rest of the body is a really effective way of capturing nature in your frame.

HOW IT WORKS

1. Cut out a square or rectangle from the cardboard. You can choose how big or small to make your frames. We tend to go for a 20cm square shape, as it is easy to hold.

2. On the cardboard, you can copy or draw a picture of your choice, but bear in mind you will be cutting part of it out, and so it is good to think about which part that might be from the start. Here are some ideas:

   - A face or self-portrait and cut out the hair
   - A mountain range and cut out the snowy tops
   - A princess and cut out a large part of the dress
   - A house and cut out the roof and/or windows
   - The face of an animal and cut out the snout or ears
   - A vase of flowers and cut out the vase or flowers
   - A simple tree and cut out the trunk
   - Letters (it is fun to do this with name initials!)

3. Take your nature frame outside and hold it up to different backgrounds. Your kids can experiment with colours, shapes and textures that are visible through the cut-outs.

4. Take a photo of the frames held up to different backgrounds as not only are these a pleasure to look at, but depending on what is in your frame, they can be printed out and used to stick on cards for family and friends.

BOTTLE BEE HOTEL

For a long time I thought that bees were very sociable little critters, swarming around in big colonies and doing their honey-making thing. It turns out they are actually quite solitary and like to nest in holes in the ground and seek refuge in small hollows. There are lots of elaborate bee hotels that you can buy, but it's really simple to make one and I'm going to show you how.

Bees are an essential part of our ecosystem and play a hugely important role in pollination, which benefits farming worldwide. The amount of pollination bees do is less now than it has been in the past and so any way to care for them is to be encouraged. By using a few commonly found materials, building a bee hotel for an outside space is enjoyable to do and also engages kids to think about how the world works around us.

WHAT YOU NEED

- A 1.5-litre plastic drinks bottle
- String, twine or ribbon
- Plain paper for drawing on
- Coloured paper or brown parcel paper
- Sticky tape
- Felt tips or colouring pencils

HOW IT WORKS

1. To make the outside of your bee hotel, cut off the top third of a large plastic bottle. The larger section with the base of the bottle will be your hotel and you can recycle the remaining third. Your base will ideally be around 25cm high.

2. Before you fill your bee hotel, you are going to decorate it on the inside of the bottle, so that your pictures are safe when it rains. On plain paper, draw and colour in small pictures of bees, or look up and print out some pictures online.

3. Cut them out and cover the reverse of the picture with sticky tape. The bottle opening should be wide enough for big or small hands to stick the pictures of the bees inside the bottle so that it looks like the bees are buzzing around inside.

4. Now gather your coloured paper, which you will roll up to make small tubes for the bees to nestle inside. Using different coloured A4 paper would be ideal, if you have it.

5. The easiest way to make the tubes is to roll the shorter side of a piece of A4 piece of paper around a pencil until you create a small tube. Pop a small piece of sticky tape on it so that it doesn't unfurl, and place inside your bottle.

6. Keep repeating the process so that you fill up your hotel with lots of paper tubes, all sitting on top of each other. This should keep small hands busy for long enough to make a cup of tea and drink it while it is hot!

7. When you've finished, wrap your string, twine or ribbon in two places towards each end of the bottle, and tie a knot to secure them in place, leaving a longer piece loose so you can hang it up.

8. Take your bee hotel outside and pick a suitable spot to hang it from, such as the branch of a tree or against a fence. Tie in place with the loose ends and enjoy the satisfaction of providing some free accommodation for any buzzy backyard visitors!

HUBBLE BUBBLE MAGIC POTIONS

I will never forget the excitement on my daughter's face after a day at an activity camp where she made magic potions. She couldn't remember anything else that she had done and was convinced there was real magic inside every jar. This activity has a special quality when using items of nature, as the earthy beauty of acorns or the delicate splendour of petals make the potions quite otherworldly. Plus, nature is free and easy to grab, making this a good option for a mindful morning or a relaxed afternoon together.

WHAT YOU NEED

- Empty plastic bottles
- Small jars or bottles with lids – a few per child
- Food colouring
- Nature items: petals, leaves, herbs, berries, nuts, clean stones
- Paper and pens
- Optional: food flavourings, biodegradable glitter, craft decorations for the bottle such as stickers, feathers, ribbon, etc.

HOW IT WORKS

1. The key to successful potion making is a little bit of grown-up preparation. Label some empty plastic bottles with imaginary potion names, such as 'witch's breath' or 'cauldron steam' and fill them three quarters full with water.

2. Drop in food colouring and bring to your desired shade. Pop the lids on and leave to one side. Make sure you pretend to your kids later on that they really are magical and you can't say where you got them from!

3. Now lay out the empty potion jars on a surface that can get messy, alongside the food flavouring, glitter and craft items if you have them. Set out the labelled potion mixtures and you're nearly ready to go.

4. Go on a nature hunt with your kids to find leaves, petals, small stones and twigs for stirring. Tell your kids to touch, smell and observe nature carefully and safely so that they can really focus on what they want to use. My tip is to wash anything grubby before using it.

5. For each type of nature, ask your kids to give it a name or a magical property so that when it goes in the water, it has a power.

6. Now you can sit back and let your kids start to mix their potions and decorate their jars as they wish. If they can, ask them to write down the recipe for each of their potions as they are making it from which you can create a family potion book.

TOP TIP: Pop some food flavourings into your next supermarket shop, for example mint, lemon and vanilla. In addition to their uses in baking and home-made play dough, they are perfect for magic potion making.

BUTTERFLY WINGS THREE WAYS

Fancy dress is a big thing in our home. We have a large fancy dress box with a broken lid, it is opened so often, which is full of hand-me-downs, charity shops finds and the odd item I have grudgingly bought new. I try to spend as little money as I can on fancy dress as it tends to get ruined or my kids grow so quickly it no longer fits. I'm always on the lookout for ways to explore role-play and dressing up, and making butterfly wings out of cardboard and decorating them with nature really is a simple, cost-free way of doing just that.

WHAT YOU NEED
- Thick cardboard – a delivery box is ideal
- Elastic, string, ribbon or large rubber bands
- Double-sided tape and/or sticky back plastic
- A sharp pencil

TOP TIP: Sticky back plastic is great for repairing torn books, sealing home-made cards, laminating DIY bookmarks and so on. Buy a large roll and don't look back. I'm sure you'll use it all and be grateful you had it to hand.

HOW IT WORKS

1. Take your cardboard and use sharp scissors to cut out the shape of butterfly wings – the bigger, the better. If you don't have enough cardboard to make one big pair of wings, you can make two individual wings and attach them firmly in the middle with sticky tape.

2. Make loops for your kids' arms by sticking down the elastic, string, ribbon or rubber bands. We found this worked best with elastic as the wings stayed on a bit better.

3. With your cardboard wings ready, you can now have fun attaching items of nature to them. Here are three simple ways we've tried and enjoyed.

   CUT-OUT WINGS: Draw a few different shapes on the main part of your wings and cut them out. On one side, attach sticky back plastic to cover the holes. Take your wings outside and choose things to stick onto the plastic such as leaves, petals, flower stems, berries and so on. When you are done, attach another piece of sticky back plastic over them on the exposed side and you will have a pair of nature wings with a cool stained-glass effect.

   PENCIL PUNCH WINGS: Using a sharp pencil, punch holes through your wings. You can do this in a pattern, swirly lines or shapes, or just at random. Without the need for any adhesive, take your wings outside and look for nature that can be poked through the holes. We did this with dandelions and it looked wonderful.

   STICK-ON WINGS: This is a simpler version of the cut-out wings, as all you need to do is cut lines of double-sided tape and stick them to the wings, peel off the backing strips and let your kids hunt for nature items to stick on. You could put your kids' initials on the wings, go for simple shapes, or just lots of strips at random.

TERRARIUM MINI GARDEN

A terrarium is like an aquarium. But instead of fish, you include soil and plants that will sit neatly in a glass jar. They look good, can be given as gifts and are incredibly fashionable. I can't stress how simple this is. If you have a recycled jar or large plastic drinks bottle, you're good to go. When I've made them with my kids, we make it up as we go along and the results have been great as the focus is on having fun, not creating a perfect micro garden. However, terrariums can be taken very seriously and there is a whole world of advice on how to make the perfect terrarium. In a nutshell, all you need to do is layer up rocks and soil and top with plants. It is hard to get this one wrong, and if it doesn't quite go according to plan, just tip it out and start again, leaving all the mess outside.

TOP TIP: These make great gifts and can easily be made seasonal such as by including acorns in autumn or holly in the winter. They look great with a brown parcel tag attached with a message too.

WHAT YOU NEED

- A glass jar (the bigger the better) or a large plastic drinks bottle
- Soil – potting compost is great, however we sourced ours from the garden
- Small stones – we collected ours on a walk
- Sand – this is preferable but not essential
- Plants, grass, shrubs, succulents – whatever you have

HOW IT WORKS

1 If you're using a jar, make sure it is clean and dry. If you're using a bottle, cut around it, approximately one third up from the bottom. Place the larger, top half to one side as you'll be using this later.

2. If you have sand, pour a layer into the bottom of your jar or bottle so it is around a centimetre deep.

3. Next place your small stones on top of the sand and pile them up so that they are around a centimetre deep. Make sure they go right up to the edge as they are nice to see through the sides.

4. Get your kids to pour or spoon your soil on top of the stones until it is about 5cm in depth and pat it down gently to form a flat surface. If you're using a tall jar, you can go as high as you like so that hands can easily get inside to do the planting.

5. Now your kids can 'plant' whatever nature they would like to in their micro garden. Encourage them to think about what will work and how it will grow. This works best if you can actually plant roots into the soil. Bits of moss can be placed around plants and if you have any colourful beads, buttons or flat marbles, you can position them to catch the light.

6. If you're using a bottle, now take the top third that you put to one side and slot it inside the bottom half, so that the rims overlap. If using a jar you can now pop the lid on.

7. Place your terrarium away from direct sunlight and spritz with water every week or so to keep the plants alive for as long as possible.

COFFEE ROCK TREASURE EGGS

This is what I call an 'input-output' activity. By this I simply mean, inputting a bit of time in the making of the activity will lead to a lot of seriously fun play – the output. In this activity, you will be making a quick mixture that you pack tightly around small toys or 'treasure', bake in the oven briefly and then hide around your garden or in an open outdoor space. The challenge is for your kids to go on a treasure hunt to find the eggs and then smash them open to retrieve the toys.

WHAT YOU NEED

Any cup works to make this mixture, just use the same one throughout. If you have more than one child, it would make sense to double the recipe.

- 1 cup plain flour
- 1 cup ground coffee (or used coffee grounds, to reduce waste)
- 1 cup sand
- Just over half a cup of salt
- Half a cup of water
- A handful of small toys (palm-sized or smaller)

TOP TIP: Coffee shops usually compost or throw away used coffee grounds and when we've asked for some for this activity, we've always found them to be very happy to help.

HOW IT WORKS

1. The first thing to do is to make your mixture. Put all the dry ingredients into a large mixing bowl and give it a good stir with a wooden spoon to combine.

2. Now slowly add in the water until the mixture is a crumbly dough and not too wet or sticky.

3. Get your kids to scoop out a generous tablespoon-sized amount of mixture and flatten it slightly in the palm of their hands. Place a small toy in the middle of the mixture and then repeat this step, scooping out more mixture and flattening it on top of the toy.

4. Ask your kids to add pressure to the ball of mixture with the toy inside, using their hands to do so. Press until the mixture has formed a ball and then pop on a baking tray and repeat with the next toy.

5. You can leave the eggs to air dry, but this takes a few days. If you can't wait, you can pop them in the oven for half an hour on each side at 180° C and they will harden.

6. Remove from the oven and leave them to cool (ideally overnight so that they totally dry out).

7. This is the really fun part. Hide your coffee rock treasure eggs around your garden or an outside space and send your kids off to hunt for them. They can they use their hands or any objects they can find to help break them open. They will crumble away and the toy can be retrieved.

8. You can turn this into a game by counting how long it takes to find them or seeing who can find them the quickest.

DANDELION HONEY

Ask your kids where they think dandelions got their name. Not only will you be encouraging them to be imaginative, but more importantly, you can sound highly knowledgeable when you tell them it comes from the French 'dent de lion', meaning lion's tooth. Dandelions make the most delicious honey – or rather syrup – which happens to be vegan, and the good news is that this recipe uses the whole head of the flower, so no petal picking is required. Dandelion honey has been consumed for centuries and dandelions also make great wine, though perhaps not so suitable as a children's activity! Dandelions are most common from March to June, and so this is an activity to bookmark for doing then.

WHAT YOU NEED
- 3 heaped cups of dandelion heads
- 350ml water
- 350g sugar
- 1 lemon, sliced

> TOP TIP: Make this in batches, as jars of dandelion honey make a fantastic gift with a home-made label and a recipe for how to use or bake with it.

HOW IT WORKS

1. The first step, as you would expect, is to pick your dandelions. The ideal place to do this is an open space where they are in abundance and are far from pollution and any pesticides. It is important to leave plenty behind, as they are a vital food source for mini beasts and also for bees.

2. Get your kids to pull the heads off the stalks of the dandelions and place them in a colander. Give them a thorough wash in cold water to ensure that they are clean.

3. Place the dandelion heads, water and lemon slices in a pan. Bring to the boil and then reduce the heat and simmer for around 15 minutes.

4. Leave the mixture to cool overnight in the pan. There is no need to refrigerate. This step will allow the flavours to infuse and lead to a beautiful floral-tasting honey at the end.

5. The next day, strain the mixture through a muslin or clean tea towel, retaining all of the liquid in a container below. Press the dandelion heads and lemon in the muslin or tea towel to ensure you have all those strong drops at the end, which are loaded with flavour.

6. Put the strained liquid back in the saucepan and warm up slowly, mixing in the sugar as you do and stirring until it is all dissolved. Bring to the boil and simmer for 15 minutes; however, do keep a close eye. You don't want your honey to crystallize, and so when the colour goes darker and the consistency is more gloopy, that is probably the time to take it off the heat.

7. Transfer into clean jam or mason jars and pop on the lid whilst the honey is still warm. When it is cool, your dandelion honey is ready to enjoy on bread, cereal, yoghurt, in salads, in baking and so on.

FAT CAKE BIRD FEEDER

Growing up, we kept binoculars by the window so that if there was an interesting bird outside, we could take a closer look. And whilst I know next to nothing about birds, I do find it fun to watch them play in a birdbath or peck at some food, not knowing they are being observed.

There are lots of different ways to make bird feeders with your kids, but this one is a firm favourite as it works every time. The steps are super simple and even my littlest one can easily join in. The 'fat' in fat cakes comes from the lard (or vegetarian alternative) that is used to bind the ingredients together, and using a yoghurt pot for a mould will show your kids how to easily reuse and recycle.

TOP TIP: Position your bird feeder somewhere that you will naturally see it when you look out of a window, so that you can easily spy on any birds or animals who stop for a nibble.

WHAT YOU NEED

The ratio for the mixture should be one part
lard to two parts dry ingredients

- A yoghurt pot per child
- String
- 1 cup (any) of lard or vegetarian substitute
- 2 cups (any) of bird food
- Handful of sultanas
- Handful of oats

HOW IT WORKS

1. Make a hole in the bottom of each yoghurt pot with some sharp
   scissors. Poke the string through the hole and tie a double knot in
   the bottom. Leave about 30cm above the yoghurt pot, to tie up
   the fat cake later.

2. Now soften your lard or veggie substitute by putting it in a glass
   bowl in the microwave for 20 seconds on a medium setting. It
   should be soft enough to be pliable but not melted, so don't be
   tempted to overcook it.

3. Pour all the dry ingredients into the bowl with the lard and get
   your kids to mix it all together with their hands. They can have
   fun squeezing the bird food through their fingers and making
   sure it is all mixed in.

4. With a spoon, transfer the mixture into your yoghurt pots so
   that they are nearly full. Ask your kids to press the mixture down
   firmly to make sure it has filled any gaps.

5. Place in the fridge for an hour or so, or in the freezer if you can't
   wait that long, and let your fat cakes harden.

6. When they have hardened, cut open the yoghurt pots down one
   side and underneath, pop out the fat cake and enjoy choosing
   your spot outside to hang it up by its string.

THE GREAT INDOORS

Going out with kids, even for a quick dash to the shops, can leave you (and by you, I mean me) feeling like you've just packed for a holiday. The famous 'bag' that comes out and about with us is laden with kit and packed for every possible eventuality. You never know when you'll need a jigsaw, three spare changes of clothes, a whole packet of tangerines or a full set of felt-tip pens. And that's just for my husband (*wink*). It's in my nature to plan, and yet I always forget something, usually the thing I need most. And why do my water bottles always leak? And why have the wet wipes I've packed suddenly dried up, particularly when I have a nappy disaster on my hands, literally?

This chapter encourages you to ditch the bag and stay home. Turn where you live into a place to visit and enjoy. The ideas here are not prescriptive; consider them more like pick and mix. Take the ones you like and ditch the ones you don't. Your kids may have their own ways to interpret them too, or come up with their own. And if this is the case, that's amazing, as it is always great when kids naturally take the lead.

HOME-MADE VILLAGE FETE

I'm a big fan of the classic village fete, even though I somehow spend more money at them than I dare acknowledge, and I never quite dress appropriately and always end up being far too hot or much too cold. The village fete is rooted in British history and culture and started out as a way for people to trade goods in the Middle Ages, moving into the present day, where the focus is much more celebratory. If you have had the pleasure of visiting a fete, I'm sure you have a few likes and dislikes and the good thing about having your own fete at home is that you can include only the elements that float your boat. Below is a list of things I find fun; feel free to add in your own.

BUNTING

This might seem low on the list of priorities, but you can get your kids to buy into their fete before it even starts. All you need is triangles of paper (fold A4 paper and cut several at once to save time), a hole punch (one either side of the long end of the triangle) and some string. Your kids can paint or decorate the triangles and even make up a name for the fete itself.

SPLAT THE RAT

This game does not get old. If you haven't played it with your family yet, you're missing a trick, because it's hilarious. The aim of the game is to splat someone on the face with a wet sponge from a distance. You can keep a tally of how successful each family member is and take it in turns to be splatted. Just make sure you use soft sponges and you have a change of clothes! We made our own soft sponges for this by cutting up strips of cellulose cleaning sponges and fastening them together in the middle with an elastic band to form a star shape. They held less water and we had more of them, which was handy.

RAFFLE

Get your kids to make raffle tickets with small rectangular pieces of paper by duplicating numbers and keeping them in two separate bags. Whoever is involved in your fete can then donate items to be won – the idea is not necessarily to keep the items, but you never know! Label each prize with its rank in the raffle, such as first, second, third prize and so on. Share out the raffle tickets amongst the participants from one of the bags and nominate someone to pull out the winning numbers from the other bag of tickets. Enjoy the excitement as each number is pulled out and let your kids have fun with their new belongings.

HOOPLA

This is a family classic that is super easy to set up and a great game for all ages. The challenge is to toss hoops over poles. Each player gets a set number of hoops and you can keep score of how many they successfully throw. You can make hoops out of card and the poles can be sticks in the ground or small drinks bottles weighed down. The humble butternut squash also makes an excellent pole if you cut off the bottom to make it flat, but be warned, you'll have rather a lot of squash to eat after you've finished playing.

GUESS HOW MANY JAR

The beauty of this activity is that you can get your kids to count whatever goes in your jar beforehand – which in my experience takes a lot of time. I've seen this done with sweets; however, a cheaper way that avoids the sugar is to use dried pasta or a cereal like Cheerios. Make sure they have a paper and a pen to keep track of what goes in. They might also like to ask family, friends or neighbours to take part and have a prize for the correct or the closest answer.

FACE-PAINTING

When I bought a palette of child-friendly face paints a while back, I would not have imagined using them as much as I have. Not only are they a quintessential part of the modern-day fete, but they can also cheer kids up when they're feeling a bit down, perk up a playdate and be a fallback when you're about to head out to the park and it begins to rain. We use face paints three ways: the grown-ups painting the kids' faces, the kids painting the grown-ups' faces and – my favourite one – the kids painting their own faces! For the last one, we prop up a mirror and supervise closely, just to make sure that eyes, noses, ears and mouths are kept face-paint free!

LET'S GO CAMPING

Camping as a family is a fun and affordable way to enjoy quality time together. However, the logistics involved can really put people off. And by people, I mean me. I've loved camping over the years but to embrace it with small kids is a different ball game entirely. And this is where the camping trip at home comes into its own. You don't need to use shared toilets, you have easy access to running water, and if your tent springs a leak, you can easily dash indoors. Here are some of the top ways that you can bring the great outdoors in and enjoy a camping trip without leaving your own front door.

TENT

If you have a tent, now is the time to use it, whether you choose to camp outside or inside your home. As you don't need to worry about packing, you can fill your tent with whatever you like, such as cushions, blankets and soft toys, as well as the more obvious items that you'll need like a sleeping bag and pillow. If you don't have a tent, I know families who have slept on their trampolines overnight all snuggled up under some duvets, although it is advisable to check the weather forecast beforehand.

CAMPFIRE SNACKS

One of my favourite things about camping is the food! And I don't mean soggy sandwiches, I mean the delicious delights you can warm up on a campfire. Depending on your outside space, setting up a barbecue is a great way to enjoy some rustic food, as is using a camping stove if you have one. You can make your own campfire, although this is not for the faint-hearted and it is important to research the best way to do it safely.

- MARSHMALLOWS: The quintessential camping snack is the toasted marshmallow and they are heavenly to eat when slightly melted on the inside and slightly crispy on the outside. You can toast marshmallows over a campfire or barbecue, and a disposable barbecue or tea lights set up on a foil-covered tray work well and require much less effort. If marshmallows aren't your thing, sprinkling some pineapple chunks with brown sugar and toasting those on a skewer is also a real treat.

- TRAIL MIX: This is traditionally a combination of dried fruits and granola which you can snack on outdoors, but we like to make our own by pouring a combination of our favourite breakfast cereals into a zip-lock bag with some chocolate chips. Popcorn, nuts, raisins, pretzels and coconut flakes all work well too, and your kids might enjoy making their own trail mix with whatever you have in the cupboard!

- HOT DOGS: These have got to be one of the simplest camping meals ever and your kids can help cook the sausages, with grown-up supervision, of course! Take your sausage (meat, vegetarian or vegan) and pop a skewer inside it, lengthways if you are going to toast it over a barbecue or campfire, or just it place on a barbecue grill. When they are thoroughly cooked, have fun squiggling sauce of your choice over the top when the sausage is safely nestled inside your roll. Yum.

HOT DRINKS

No camping trip is complete without a flask of hot chocolate! My kids are huge hot chocolate fans and whilst ready-made powder is fine, we like to make our own. It is really simple to do and you can use cocoa powder but we go all out and use real chocolate chunks. Heat up milk in a saucepan until it is simmering and add in chunks of whatever chocolate you fancy – white, milk, dark, mint-flavoured, orange-flavoured and so on. Stir until it is all melted and serve or pour into a flask for later.

SING-SONGS AND STORYTIME

If you imagine a scene from a film involving a camping trip, I am sure it conjures up an image of sitting around a campfire, telling stories and singing songs. There is no reason why you can't do this at home, involving your kids from the outset. You might like them to create a camping playlist that you can listen to, organize a singalong of songs you all know, or even make up a new song. Stories can help get your kids ready to snuggle down, and so have a stash of books to read that your kids can choose from. And if you can, let your imagination run wild and make some stories up!

BEATING THE BUGS

If you're camping outside in the summer, you do run the risk of coming eye to eye with a bug or two. There are plenty of products on the market to repel insects, especially those that bite. But if you'd like to make your own, you can bunch together some sprigs of sage, mint and lavender and secure with string. Not only do these smell gorgeous, but if you pop them on your camping stove, barbecue or campfire, the smell of them smouldering should keep the bugs well away.

OFF TO THE SEASIDE

There are few things I love more than a trip to the seaside – to feel the sand between my toes, the cool sea breeze and get a whiff of fish and chips, all with an ice cream in my hand. This is, however, a luxury for us, living well over an hour away from the nearest coast. And so if you can't bring the kids to the coast, why not bring the coast to your kids for the day? It won't be quite the same, but it will be fun and it's an easy way to spruce up a warm day outside or inject some summer fun indoors.

SAND

Nothing feels quite the same as sinking your feet into cold sand on a hot day, but playing with sand is still a firm favourite with kids and if you have a sandpit at home, now is the time to use it. If you don't have a sandpit, you can fill a plastic tub or washing basket with sand and pop in some play equipment like a bucket, spade and sand moulds. Kitchen utensils also work well for sand play and a potato masher is great for sand printing. You could hide coins or small toys in the sand before you start to turn sand play into an excavation exercise. Using small stones and twigs, you can make patterns, shapes or even pretend dinosaur skeletons on the surface.

SEA

Getting into swimming gear without the faff of doing it awkwardly behind a towel is definitely a bonus of being at home! Whilst swimming in the sea is not something you can replicate at home, playing in the paddling pool is a close second. If you want to keep water mess to a minimum, fill your bath tub with water and any suitable toys, especially the sea or fish related ones. You can turn the bath water blue with a little blue food colouring (don't worry, it doesn't stain if it's really diluted) or buy some blue Gelli Baff to make water play even more fun, although I don't recommend using this goo mix outside.

ICE CREAM

You can recreate some of the magic of visiting a beachside ice cream stand by fashioning your own ice cream station at home. A few different flavours of ice cream, some cones and a variety of toppings will not only occupy your kids but deliver on flavour too, with very little hassle. You can also make your own no-churn ice cream by beating together 200g of sweetened condensed milk, 600ml of double cream and a splash of vanilla flavouring. When it is a thick, creamy consistency, put it inside a lidded tub and freeze until solid. A really simple vegan alternative is to mix a tin of coconut milk with a generous tablespoon of vanilla flavouring and freeze in ice lolly moulds. My kids love these and don't notice that they are essentially sugar free.

SEASIDE PHOTO SHOOT

This is a great idea for a rainy day and for any kids who don't fancy sand or water. The challenge is to create a beach scene on the floor with items that you have around your home and then take a photo from above to capture it in full. You can use blue towels, sheets or blankets for the sea, scrunched up yellow clothing for the sand, leaves from outside as your seaweed – the possibilities are endless.

BEACH GAMES

There is no shortage of beach games available to buy, but you don't need to spend money to make things fun at home.

- BEACH BALL VOLLEYBALL: Blow-up beach balls are great and can be used for all sorts of play although they work really well for volleyball – they're so big, they are hard to miss! My top tip is to buy two at a time, leaving one in the car or in a day bag for when you're out and about.

- BALLOON TENNIS: This is an easy alternative to beach volleyball and great if you have some leftover balloons lying around. If you don't have tennis rackets, fly swatters or even paper plates are also great to use.

- SAND NOUGHTS AND CROSSES: Simply use your sandpit, or even some salt on a tray to play a simple game of noughts and crosses by making lines in the grains.

- BEACH TOWEL LIMBO: Roll up a beach towel lengthways so that you have a tube and use it as a limbo stick! Two people hold each end and the players have to lean back and limbo underneath it.

- INUKSHUK: This is an Inuit word to describe the stone towers that were traditionally used as markers on journeys. Beaches often have lots of stones around and so it's a great game to try. All you need to do is collect as many stones as you can and then create a tower by placing them on top of each other. The winner has the tallest tower, or perhaps the one that doesn't fall over straight away!

DIY SPA DAY

I didn't think my five-year-old would understand the concept of a spa day, having never discussed it before. However, when I asked her if it was something she fancied doing, she enthusiastically replied, 'Oh yes, Mum, I've always wanted to put cucumbers on my eyes.' I don't think it is ever too early to introduce the concept of wellbeing to kids, particularly if it involves an activity that the whole family can take part in and enjoy.

SPA EXPERIENCE

One of the highlights of a spa day is the experience of being in a spa environment, and a few quick hacks can help turn your home into a place of wellbeing and relaxation. Involve your kids in giving your spa a name and making a sign for it – if you have a light-up message box, this would be great to use. Working with your kids, you can create your own spa menu of treatments you'd like to have, from a long bath to a foot soak to a head massage.

THE ULTIMATE SOAK

Having some relaxation in water is a key part of any spa experience. However, it's unlikely your kids will buy into having a bath just for the sake of it. To spruce up the experience, dim the lights, play some music, have a stack of towels ready, allow your kids to put cucumber slices on their eyes and, depending on what they fancy, you can add a few drops of food colouring to the water for them to swirl around, or add extra bubble bath or Crazy Soap for a layer of foam.

FACE MASKS

There are lots of easy home-made face mask recipes you can try out containing natural ingredients that you may even have already in your fridge. Here are two recipes that we have tested and enjoyed, and which you can follow or adapt, or make up your own! It is recommended to do a patch test beforehand, to make sure that little skin won't become irritated.

CHOCOLATE FUDGE FACE MASK

- 1 avocado
- 2 tablespoons honey
- 3 tablespoons cocoa powder

Mash or whizz the avocado in a food processor until it is a fine pulp without any lumps. Mix in the cocoa and honey until it is a smooth light brown colour. Apply to the face, being careful around the eyes, nose and mouth, and leave on for up to 10 minutes. Wash off with a splash of water or a damp flannel.

STRAWBERRY BLISS FACE MASK

- 5 ripe strawberries
- 2 tablespoons fine oats
- 3 teaspoons plain yoghurt

Crush the strawberries with a fork until they make a paste. Mix in the oats and plain yoghurt and stir until well combined. The mixture should be pink and creamy! Apply to the face, being careful around the eyes, nose and mouth, and leave on for up to 10 minutes. Wash off with a splash of water or a damp flannel.

HAND MASSAGES

This is a lovely way to connect with your kids and keeps their little hands busy without them getting up to mischief. Hands are regularly used to express emotions and so it is fitting that they too get some downtime. Hand and wrist massages can help children to relax their muscles and reduce tension, as well as boosting their mood. There really is no reason not to give it a go.

- Set the scene for your kids by telling them to take some nice deep breaths and to imagine a calm place in their heads. Lay their hands on a towel on top of a cushion or pillow so that they are really comfy.

- Take one of their hands and use some baby oil, olive oil or coconut oil to massage over the whole hand and wrist in gentle strokes.

- Next, use your thumb to rub in small gentle circles around each part of the hand. Now gently squeeze each finger, applying pressure with your finger and thumb.

- Turn their hand over and walk your fingertips over the fleshy part of the hand.

- Hold their hand in yours and then repeat for the other hand.

DING DONG PIZZA DELIVERY

I have yet to meet a child who does not enjoy pizza and whenever we go out to eat as a family, pizza is always our go-to option. There is something so pleasing about the whole family enjoying the same meal and the great thing about pizzas is that they can have as few or as many toppings as you wish. Making pizza isn't complicated and I've included my favourite recipe below.

THE MENU

Scouring the menu in any pizza restaurant is always fun, even if you tend to frequent the same pizzeria like we do. Getting your kids to create their own pizza menu involves zero planning and is fun even if you don't plan on actually making any. Pizza menus are widely available to browse online and your kids may have ideas for combinations of their own. They can come up with a name for their pizza restaurant and even a logo for their pizza brand. Why not ask them to think up a dessert menu too – I heard that chocolate spread on pizza dough is especially delicious!

BEST PIZZA RECIPE EVER

I have pretty much stopped buying ready-made pizzas for my kids, as I have a fantastic recipe for an incredibly quick to make dough that is cheap and uses store-cupboard items, so I don't have to plan ahead.

- 1 sachet fast action dried yeast
- 400g plain flour
- olive oil
- 230ml warm water

1. Mix together the yeast and the flour in a bowl and make a little well in the middle.

2. Pour the water and two big glugs of olive oil into the well and stir, mix and knead into a ball of dough.

3. Tip onto a floured surface and knead, bash and poke it until you have a smooth dough that can be easily rolled and formed into shapes.

4. Top with tomato sauce and any toppings of your choice and leave for around 10 minutes so the dough has a bit of time to rise.

5. Pop in a preheated oven (200° C) and in 10 minutes or so, your pizzas will be ready.

THE DELIVERY BOX

You can add to the experience of creating your home-made pizzeria by using cardboard delivery boxes. These are cheap to buy and are a great way to incorporate some arts and crafts into your day. They can also be easily recycled at the end. Your kids can decorate the outside of the boxes and if you do make your own pizza, make sure to serve it up in the box!

STARGAZING EXTRAVAGANZA

We all know that, unlike a trip to the seaside or a visit to a pizzeria, you cannot take a day trip into space. Maybe one day, but it might be a wait. With that in mind, you can instead enjoy some intergalactic fun in the comfort of your own home and learn a few new things about the galaxy around you.

STARGAZING

Stargazing is a totally free activity for kids to try and there are a few ways to tackle some basic astronomy to make it fun for your kids. First and foremost, the darker your surroundings, the more likely you are to see things in the sky. If you have a telescope or binoculars, now is the time to use them. And you don't need to have any prior knowledge as there are plenty of apps that you can download so that you can learn together. Here are two brilliant (and free) ones:

- The Skyview app is fantastic, letting you point your device at the sky to identify galaxies, stars, constellations and satellites. You can set reminders for celestial events, follow the daily sky tracks for the sun and the moon and even use augmented reality to spot objects in the sky.

- The NASA app is really informative and lets you view over 17,000 images, watch live TV and videos, find out about upcoming sighting opportunities and access news and information. You can also set up notifications to receive a daily NASA image straight to your phone.

COSMIC SNACKS AND DRINKS

If you plan on being outdoors, you'll definitely need some snacks to keep you going, and it's amazing how many confectionery items have suitably space-themed names. Here are just a few you could add to your treat buffet: Mars Bar, Milky Way, Galaxy, Starburst and flying saucer sweets – a personal favourite of mine. For a healthier approach, cut up fruit and vegetables into small pieces, give your kids some pictures of rockets, planets or space, and let them create pictures on their plates to represent what they see.

TENNIS BALL ECLIPSE

If you want to demonstrate for your kids how a solar eclipse (where the sun is hidden by the moon) works, this is a super simple way to boost their knowledge with just a tennis ball, a football and a torch! Here, the tennis ball represents the moon, the football represents the Earth and the torch is the sun. When the torch is shone on the tennis ball first and the football behind it, a shadow will appear on the football. This is an eclipse shadow, where the moon conceals the sun.

STAR-THEMED PLAYLIST

No stargazing party is complete without a great playlist, jam-packed with space-themed songs to keep you all going. There are lots of great tracks which involve astronomy-related words, such as star, sun, moon, rocket, Venus and space. Older kids could do some research and come up with a playlist of their own, whereas younger ones could listen to a playlist and try to spot any words that relate to space. To get you started, here are a few of my favourites:

- 'Rocket Man' by Elton John
- 'Out of Space' by The Prodigy
- 'Man on the Moon' by REM
- 'Fly Me to the Moon' by Frank Sinatra
- 'Venus' by Bananarama

THE ROMAN ARMY EYE TEST

The ancient Romans devised an eye test to help them decide who could become an archer in the army – a prized role indeed. As they wanted soldiers with the best eyesight, they came up with this simple test to see who would be suitable. It involved looking at the stars at nine o'clock in the evening to see the shape of The Plough. This is a series of stars shaped like a hand-held plough – the sort that is traditionally used to cut corn by hand. On the handle of The Plough, there are three stars. The middle star is called Mizar. If you focus on Mizar, you should be able to see a second star appear next to it, called Alcor. If you could see Alcor in Roman times, it meant your eyesight was good enough, and if not, you could be demoted to a much less exciting role.

FAMSTOCK: THE FESTIVAL

Festivals have not only grown in number and popularity in recent years, but many are now geared up for families, with a vast array of events and activities to suit different ages, needs and budgets. Going to a festival is a totally unique experience and nothing can replace seeing your favourite band live on stage. Saying that, there are lots of features of festivals that can be simple and incredibly fun to replicate at home and I dare you to give it a go!

GLAMPING

In case this is new to you, glamping is 'glamorous camping', where you can combine all your creature comforts with the fun of the great outdoors. Why not try setting up camp at home, whether inside on a rainy weekend afternoon or outside on a hot summer's day? All you need is a tent, teepee or a makeshift tent made of bed sheets or similar, and you can fill it with items to make your 'stay' super comfortable, such as cushions, blankets, pillows, rugs and so on. If you have fairy or festoon lights, these look great, and your kids can go on a hunt for items they'd like to include in their luxury glamping experience!

THE LINE-UP

Every festival has a line-up of what to listen to, do and see, and this is normally what draws people to a festival in the first place. To do this at home, you could decide on a few different 'stages' and what is going to be featured on each one. You could simply make a playlist for all the music you want to listen to at your festival, or choose some clips to watch of your favourite performers playing music live.

Lots of festivals have alternative stages for things like folk music and so part of the fun could be making up your own songs with whatever instruments you have. Poetry and live storytelling are also popular at festivals and so your kids could write their own poems and stories, or help you think up some rhyming words to put on paper. Festivals also often have craft tents and so you might like to pick up an idea from the craft section of this book to try out.

FESTIVAL CLOTHING

There is something about being at a festival where you can let your inner hippie hang out. Let your kids think about wearing something a bit different that they wouldn't normally put on. You could even look into upcycling some of your existing clothing. We did this by cutting up some old T-shirts, taking off the sleeves, snipping a fringe along the bottom and changing the shape of the neckline. And if you have any white T-shirts and the right dye, a family set of tie-dyed T-shirts would look great in a picture to remember the day by.

FESTIVAL DRINKS STATION

Going to the bar for a drink is a firm festival fixture and so creating a child-friendly drinks station could be a great addition to your festival. By simply lining up different soft drinks, cups and drink accessories, your kids can have fun making up their own concoctions. Crushed ice is a great addition, as it turns most drinks into slushies. Slices of citrus fruit, cucumber and sprigs of fresh mint are a healthier way to decorate drinks, while glacé cherries, paper umbrellas and biodegradable straws all add to the experience. Even just a few drops of food colouring can turn a cup of iced water into something magical!

MINI RAVERS

Kids love to dance and one way to let them burn off some excess energy (if they have any left) is to have a mini rave. One way to make this, in the words of my own kids, 'the funnest thing ever' is to turn the lights off, give them glow sticks (cheap to buy and readily available online) and pop on some upbeat music. It really is a wondrous sight to see neon shapes dancing in the dark. You could take this one step further and use sticky tape to attach some glow sticks to the limbs of your kids, so that they become lit-up dancing skeletons. If you haven't tried this, please do, as it had us in stitches!

FAMILY MAGIC SHOW

Teaching your kids a few simple magic tricks is not only a great way to pass the time but can upskill them with the trick itself while also supporting communication skills, especially if they are a little shy. Like grown-ups, kids can struggle in social situations and so having a trick to fall back on is confidence boosting for them and fun for someone else to watch. Plus, we all need a little bit of magic in our lives, don't we?

Here are three simple tricks to try with items you're likely to have around your home. And if you do want to take it one step further, there are magic kits you can buy, plus the internet is brimming with magic hacks and more advanced tricks to try out.

THE DISAPPEARING COIN

WHAT YOU NEED
A round coin, a small piece of aluminium foil and a piece of paper.

HOW IT WORKS
1. Place a small piece of foil over the coin and press down across the top and around the edges so that you make an imprint of the coin.

2. Remove the coin and trim off any excess foil, so that you have a (quite flimsy) replica.

3. Put the foil coin in the centre of your palm and tell the audience that you are going to make it disappear.

4. Place the paper on top of your palm and say 'abracadabra'.

5. Remove the paper and let the audience see it is still there. Show frustration and try again.

6. Apologize to the audience and say the trick hasn't worked, before crumpling up the paper with the foil coin inside to make the coin disappear, much to their amazement!

THE SLICED BANANA TRICK

WHAT YOU NEED
A whole banana, a needle or sharp narrow skewer

HOW IT WORKS
1. This trick will involve grown-up help to prepare but it doesn't take away from the fun. The big reveal can be done by your kids and the gasp they will get from their audience will be a real mood booster!

2. To prepare, place the unpeeled banana on a flat surface. Choose one of the ridges of the banana that run down the skin and make sure that it is facing up.

3. Insert the needle into the banana, on the ridge, about a centimetre from the top of the fruit. Wiggle it about from side to side – this will cut through the banana on the inside without it being visible from the outside.

4. Repeat this step at 1cm intervals, down the ridge, until the banana has been fully sliced on the inside.

5. Present the unpeeled banana to an audience and explain that you have magic powers to slice the banana on the inside. Squint at the banana meaningfully for a few seconds and then peel back the skin to reveal the sliced-up banana inside.

CUP THROUGH A TABLE

WHAT YOU NEED
A plastic cup, a tea towel, a piece of Lego (or similar small toy)

HOW IT WORKS
1. Pop your toy on one side of a table with your audience facing you on the other side. Everyone should be sitting down on a chair. Place the cup over the toy and the tea towel loosely on top.

2. Explain that the cup has magic powers and can make the toy disappear if everyone concentrates hard enough on this happening.

3. Lift the cup up with the tea towel over the top and tell everyone to focus on the toy. Meanwhile, drop the cup into your lap without people seeing.

4. Now drop the tea towel onto the toy and hit the table with your hand as you do so, as if pretending to push the cup through the table.

5. At the same time, tip the cup off your lap so that it lands on the floor with a bang, as if it has fallen through.

6. Lift up the tea towel to reveal that there is no cup and tell the audience to look under the table – you couldn't make the toy disappear but you could magic away a cup!

THE BIG FAMILY

Quizzes are a brilliant way for families to get to know each other a bit better, bond and also bring out a bit of healthy competition! You don't need many resources to make different quiz rounds and involving your kids in creating quizzes is actually engaging them in a learning activity without them realizing. Quizzes are readily tailored to suit the ages and interests of your kids and it is the sort of game that can be easily played at home or even over video calls with other family members. Here are four different rounds you could create and play.

SNACKS

You'll have noticed that food features quite heavily in this chapter, and rightly so. Snacks keep kids fuelled and avoid the inevitable 'I'm hungry', which drives me up the wall. Put out some small bowls and fill them with different-flavoured crisps, or cut up some vegetables and pitta bread and serve with hummus. Having something to snack on can keep them focused on the task and avoid any 'hangry' moments that can get in the way.

FILM ROUND

We love films and regularly spend a lazy Sunday afternoon snuggled up on the sofa together, watching a film. We're also huge cinema fans and so over the years, have clocked up some decent family film knowledge!

There are a few different ways that you can play a film round. One way is to write out a list of well-known lines or quotes from films your family knows and likes. The challenge is then to match up the

lines to the films. Another way is for your kids to dress up and pose for a picture recreating a well-known scene from a film. You then use the photo to guess the film. Finally, you can simply go for some good old trivia. We did this recently using a colour theme where we had to guess what colour clothing people were wearing in different films. It was harder than you think!

MUSIC ROUND

My kids love music and we always have the radio on or something playing in the background. I've seen how they love to dance at parties and so including music in a family quiz is a must.

Make a playlist of songs from films and your kids have to guess which film the song is from and maybe, for a bonus point, the name of the person who sings it. You could alternatively start playing a well-known song and, when the music stops, your kids have to carry on singing it to get a point. Or you could quite simply opt for 'guess the intro', where you play the first ten seconds or so of a song, and your kids have to guess what it is.

CRYPTIC CONFECTIONERY ROUND

This has got to be one of my favourite quiz rounds of all time. The idea is that you make up cryptic clues to describe chocolate bars or sweets. It involves a play on words and you can either get your kids to help you make up the cryptic clues or you can come up with them for a really engaging round of questions. It is best to start with a list of confectionery that's familiar to your family and take it from there.

Here are some examples to give you an idea:
- Clever people = Smarties
- Talk very quietly = Wispa Bar
- It's party time = Celebrations
- A piece of snow = Flake
- Spinning around = Twirl

TRUE! FALSE!

TRUE OR FALSE

One of the challenges with a quiz involving trivia is that it can end up leaving kids feeling like they don't know enough. Knowledge recall is challenging at the best of times and my feeling is that a good quiz leaves players feeling upbeat. A true or false round is a great way to get kids thinking and this simple way of answering questions means the quiz can move at a good pace. Here are some examples of the kinds of true or false rounds your kids might enjoy:

FOOD: What is the main ingredient in certain foods; which countries do different foods originate from; or where do different fruit and vegetables grow (in the ground, on a vine, on a tree).

COUNTRIES: The capital cities of different countries; what continents different countries are in (you could look at a map beforehand); and what languages are spoken in different countries.

ANIMALS: Where animals normally live; what do animals normally eat; what is the fastest, tallest, heaviest animal in the animal kingdom.

FAMILY MEMBERS: Your kids can ask family members for facts about them to include in a true or false quiz, such as their favourite food, best subject at school, favourite book or about an event that happened to them when they were growing up.

ONE MORE THING

I know you want the best for your kids and I'm sure you want to spark curiosity in them about the world they live in. I'm also confident that you want your kids to grow up asking questions and, rather than fear getting the answer wrong, have enthusiasm for finding out what the right answer is. Simply by asking questions and researching answers with your kids, whether in a structured or unstructured way, you'll be helping them to appreciate that knowledge is a journey and sometimes even the grown-ups don't have all the answers.

AFTERNOON TEA

There is nothing I don't like about afternoon tea. I mean, what is there not to like about an additional meal in the day, consisting mostly of cake, where it's totally acceptable to have seconds, or even thirds! My kids have grown up having tea with family and friends at the weekend and on occasion, we've tried going out for afternoon tea as a family, although it often tends to be more hassle than it is worth. I find the tea spillages, jam-smeared hands, cutlery falling on the floor and endlessly needing to get up and take my toddler for a 'walk' stressful to say the least. So tea at home is the way to go. It isn't expensive, it's totally delicious and there are plenty of ways to get your kids involved to make it fun for all the family.

TABLE DECORATION

A big part of the fun of afternoon tea is the experience of sitting at a table that looks different to ordinary mealtimes. Whilst eating a sandwich or a slice of cake is not necessarily that memorable, combine these with a beautifully laid out table and you have an event on your hands. And you don't need to spend money on tiered cake plates, tablecloths or fancy napkins (although if you do want to do this, don't let me stand in your way). Your kids can help you design, decorate and lay the table with whatever you already have. Plain paper napkins can be decorated with felt-tip pens, menus can be written out on paper, nature can be picked and popped in a vase, place-names can be made with a bit of card, and favourite clothes put on, all helping to create some afternoon tea magic.

SANDWICHES

A sandwich done well really is a thing of great joy and the variety of fillings is endless. It is a staple food for kids and one of the quickest things to put together for an out and about lunch. It is also one of the most versatile of foods, as you can easily change the bread, the filling and the shape of the sandwiches. Plus making a sandwich is something your kids can help you do, so long as you can cope with some wonky spreading!

Why not plan some new sandwich combinations with your kids? Ask them to describe their dream sandwich or look up some sandwich filling combinations online and design a menu. We've enjoyed toasted cheese and tomato sandwiches, fish-finger rolls with mayonnaise and ketchup, and bagels topped with peanut butter. While you can stick to the more traditional afternoon tea fillings of sliced cucumber or egg mayonnaise, there is absolutely no pressure to. If your kids like the food, everyone will enjoy it more.

LEMONADE SCONES

No afternoon tea is complete without scones topped with cream and jam. I am aware of the big debate around what you put on first, the cream or the jam. Personally, I put the cream on first, simply because I make a terrible mess the other way round, so please don't hold it against me!

Scones are incredibly easy to make and in my experience rarely go wrong. Here is a recipe with only three main ingredients, one of which is lemonade! They are quick, delicious, and don't require any weighing, and I've yet to meet a child who hasn't enjoyed them.

Ingredients:
Pick a small mug and use this for all the measurements
- 3 ½ mugs of self-raising flour
- 1 mug double cream
- 1 mug lemonade (any will do)

Method:
1. Preheat your oven to 180°C and line a baking tray with baking or greaseproof paper. Put all the ingredients into a large bowl and mix with a wooden spoon until you have a sticky dough.

2. Tip the dough onto a floured surface and knead a few times until it is less sticky and easily moulds into a ball. Knead the dough as little as you can. Too much kneading can make the scones less fluffy.

3. Pat the dough down until it is 2–3cm thick. You can use a rolling pin if you like, but don't press down too hard.

4. Take a cutter and press it down into the dough to make the scones. We use a fluted round cutter but any shape will do.

5. Lift the scones onto the baking tray and brush the tops with a bit of milk. Bake in the oven for 15 minutes until golden.

6. Take out of the oven and transfer to a cooling rack. Place a tea towel over the top to keep them from going hard. Serve slightly warm with as much butter, cream or jam as you wish.

AFTERNOON TEA GAMES

One of the great pleasures of afternoon tea is the sense of calm
that comes from sitting down at a nicely laid table with a cup of tea
in your hand. However, when you have kids, this is rather less likely,
and so here are some afternoon tea games to keep them occupied.

TEA TRAY MEMORY GAME

Grab a tray and place an assortment of items on it, some big, some
small and ideally in different colours. The game is to give your kids
a set period of time to memorize what is on the tray and then ask
them to recall what was on it, either by writing it down, drawing the
items out on paper or simply telling you as much as they can. Your
kids could even challenge you to a round.

PIN THE HANDLE ON THE TEAPOT

You'll need two pieces of paper or card, one big and one small.
Draw a teapot on the large one, and on the small one draw a
handle for the teapot. Cut the handle out and put a blob of Blu-Tack
in the middle. Attach your teapot to a wall or flat surface, blindfold
your kids with a scarf or tie, and give the first player the teapot
handle. Carefully spin them round three times and then ask them
to stick down the handle where they think it ought to go. Make a
mark where each handle went and whoever was the most accurate
is the winner.

TEABAG TOSS

This is one for the grown-ups as much as the kids! Take a handful
of teabags (five or more) and wet them slightly, squeezing out any
drips so that they are damp. On the floor, line up some plastic cups
and pop a pencil on the floor around a metre or so away from the
cups to act as the starting line. Give each player five bags and the
aim is to see how many they can toss into the cups. Keep a tally of
how many each player successfully gets in, or forget about winning
and just have some fun!

WELLBEING WONDERS

Wellbeing is a term that is regularly bandied about but often misunderstood. The simplest way that I have found to explain it is quality of life and our state of happiness. Feelings of wellbeing are fundamental to our overall health and so it is great to embrace this with our kids. Having practical strategies for children to make sense of their emotions and the world around them is easier said than done. With this in mind, I have compiled a list of five easy ideas here that I hope you enjoy doing with your kids and, just as importantly, will help them to lead happy little lives.

S'NO PROBLEM
SNOW GLOBE

Making a snow globe is incredibly quick and easy. So much so that the aim of this activity is not the craft involved but the watching and reflecting on the end result. Once you've explained to your kids how a snow globe can help them make sense of their feelings and emotions, they will have a go-to object that they made themselves whenever they need a bit of calm.

THE WELLBEING BIT: The idea is that a snow globe represents the mind. When we have lots going on in our heads, it is like the snow globe has been shaken up and there is a blizzard. Emotions, worries and dealing with the unexpected are all things that can cause our 'blizzard' to happen. However, by simply imagining the blizzard dispersing and disappearing, we can help to calm our minds. Explain this to your kids, using your own words to do so. You might even like to ask them to close their eyes and imagine this happening.

WHAT YOU NEED

- A jam jar, or equivalent sized jar
- Small plastic toys
- Superglue or hot glue
- Food colouring
- Snow: this can be made up of crushed eggshell, biodegradable glitter, sequins, or small cut-up pieces of foil

HOW IT WORKS

1. Take the lid off the clean, empty jar. Choose a small plastic toy or plastic item that can go inside. As the toy will be submerged in water, it should ideally be plastic.

2. Stick the toy inside the jar at the bottom. Some people suggest sticking it to the inside of the lid, however my jars have always leaked when I've done this. Leave the glue to harden and dry.

3. Meanwhile, prepare your snow. There are a few ways to do this, but my personal favourite is using foil. Take a piece of foil and cut it into long, thin strips. Then have your kids snip the strips into tiny pieces into a bowl. You can also crush up eggshell in a zip-lock bag with a rolling pin. Or if you have craft items at home, hunt out any sequins, biodegradable glitter or other items that are suitable for immersing in water.

4. Fill your jar with cold water, leaving a centimetre or two at the top. Cool boiled water is ideal as it is likely to be a bit clearer, but it is not essential.

5. Let your kids drop in some food colouring – we like to use blue for this, as it is a cool, calm colour.

6. Screw the lid on the top of the snow globe as tightly as you can and slowly turn it around so that the lid is now at the bottom. Let your kids give it a vigorous shake and watch the food colouring, water and snow combine.

GRATITUDE TREE

I'm pretty sure that if I asked you what you wanted for your kids in the future, your answer would feature the word 'happiness'. This activity is one for all the family and it is a great way for you to model to your kids how to be thankful. The aim is to place leaves (luggage tags) on a tree (bouquet of sticks) and in doing so create a physical representation of the things you are grateful for.

THE WELLBEING BIT: The link between gratitude, or being thankful, and our happiness has been well researched and so we know that expressing gratitude makes us feel more positive. Expressing gratitude can also improve our physical health, our self-esteem, our ability to deal with challenges, and the way that we relate to others. It has even been suggested that it can help us sleep better.

WHAT YOU NEED
- A generous handful of sticks
- Luggage or gift tags
- String, twine or ribbon
- A vase or jug

HOW IT WORKS

1. Gather together your sticks like a bouquet of flowers. Ideally your sticks will be of similar height to cut flowers that you can buy in the shops.

2. Tie some string, twine or ribbon around the middle, or simply put them in a vase or jug.

3. Now gather your luggage or gift tags and some pens. This is the most important bit. Your kids write something they are grateful for on each gift tag and hang it on your stick tree. If your kids can't write yet, let them tell you and you can write it down.

4. Put your gratitude tree somewhere central in your house. We put ours on the kitchen table for a few days and used it as a talking point over dinner. My five-year-old put on some of her own leaves of gratitude without me seeing, which made me think that it had all been worthwhile.

Gratitude can be about anything. But to get you started, here are some useful prompts:

- Family or friends
- A quality or talent that you have
- Something in nature or outside
- A hobby or something you love to do
- Something you love to eat or drink
- Something you've learnt this year
- Something you love about where you live

SUPER SQUISHY STRESS BALL

Not so long ago, I took my older daughter to one of those shops where everything costs one pound. I gave her a one-pound coin and said that she could – within reason – pick what she wanted. We scoured the whole shop before she settled on a small squishy toy, which in my view was worth much less than the coin in her hand. 'Are you sure you want this?' I asked, thinking about all the jigsaws, dolls and craft items we had walked past. 'Yes, because I just love squishing' was her reply. Kids love to squish and it is good for them too. Rather than visiting the pound shop, you can simply add flour to an empty balloon to make as many squishy stress balls as you wish.

THE WELLBEING BIT: There are a lot of nerves in our hands that are connected to the brain. When we put pressure on a stress ball, it gives our nerves and muscles a bit of a workout. This not only improves the functioning of our nervous system but also helps to alleviate stress in a natural way.

WHAT YOU NEED

- Balloons – thick latex ones are ideal
- A small, empty plastic bottle
- A cup of flour (any) per stress ball
- Optional: dried lavender or lavender oil

HOW IT WORKS

1. Take the lid off your empty bottle and if you have a funnel, insert that into the top of the bottle. If you don't, you can make your own by rolling some paper into the shape of an ice cream cone and holding it in place with some sticky tape.

2. Let your kids help you decant around a cup of flour into the bottle. It should be just over half full, or thereabouts.

3. Take the funnel out of the bottle. If you're using lavender oil or dried lavender to add a calming smell to your stress balls, add in the petals or couple of drops into the flour now. Making sure you cover the open bottle top, give your bottle a shake to mix everything up.

4. Take your balloon and place the neck over the top of the open bottle. When it feels securely in place, ask your kids to help you tip the bottle upside down so that the flour pours into the balloon. Press your fingers around the neck of the bottle to keep the balloon in place and shake any remaining flour into the balloon.

5. Peel the top of the balloon off the bottle and tie in a knot so that the flour has no way of escaping!

6. Your squishy stress ball is now ready and can be decorated with felt-tip pens such as Sharpies, or have wool or string tied around the knot to be hair. We've attached stick-on googly eyes before, however they can get in the way.

7. Remind your kids to be careful not to put the balloons down on anything sharp, as you don't want them to burst!

LOLLY STICK WORRY DOLLS

Worry dolls are a Guatemalan tradition where children tell their worries to small hand-crafted dolls and then place them under their pillows before they go to sleep at night. When they wake up in the morning, the idea is that the dolls have given them the knowledge and wisdom to deal with their worries. You can easily make your own version of worry dolls with lolly sticks and a few craft items, giving your children a strategy to help deal with the difficult emotions they experience.

THE WELLBEING BIT: Being able to articulate your emotions and voice worries or concerns is an important life skill. A worry doll does not have feelings of its own and can be a trustworthy listener for a child to be able to share how they are feeling. Putting feelings into words can help take worries away and reduce anxiety, both in children and also in grown-ups.

WHAT YOU NEED

- Lolly sticks –I prefer jumbo lolly sticks, but regular ones work too
- Wool in a few different colours
- Pipe cleaners
- Card (delivery box card is ideal, but any will do)
- Felt-tip pens

HOW IT WORKS

1. Cut out a few circles from your card, approximately a thumbprint in size.

2. Let your kids draw faces on the circles of card with felt tips, making sure the main features are really clear.

3. The next step is to attach a pipe cleaner to the lolly stick three quarters of the way up – these will be the arms of your doll. Using glue or sticky tape, attach the pipe cleaner to the back of your lolly stick and cut the arms down to size.

4. Now it is time to wrap your lolly sticks in wool. Take the end of your wool and stick it to the back of the lolly stick, about 1cm from the top. Wrap the wool around the lolly stick, nice and tightly so that it stays in place. Go over and around where your pipe cleaner arms are so that they poke out of the wool on either side.

5. When you want to finish using a particular colour of wool, snip the wool and tie it with a small knot to a strand wound above it and trim off any excess.

6. To finish off your worry dolls, stick on the cardboard cut-out faces that you have already prepared and leave to dry until they are secure. And don't forget to leave them near to where your kids sleep so that they are ready to help when any worries creep in.

ORIGAMI FORTUNE TELLER

This fortune teller is made of origami, which is the art of folding paper to make different shapes. They have been played with by children for centuries and you may well have come across them before by a different name, such as cootie catcher, chatterbox or paku-paku. By folding a square piece of paper in a few different directions and placing it over your forefinger and thumb, you will create a hand game where players pick options that lead them to an outcome. In this case, the fortune teller will reveal a hidden wellbeing strategy to try out.

THE WELLBEING BIT: Strategies to promote wellbeing and mental health are a constructive way to help children cope with their emotions. Our mental health, a bit like our physical health, is something we should invest in, as good mental health can help us to feel better and have positive relationships with the people around us. Equipping children with practical ways to look after their mental health can help them deal not only with the present, but with difficult situations in the future.

WHAT YOU NEED

• Plain A4 paper

• Pen or pencil

• Scissors

HOW IT WORKS

1. Take your paper and fold the bottom of the paper to the side of the page so that you make a triangle shape.

2. Fold your square in half to make a folded line that crosses the existing one. This will show you where the centre of your square is. Snip or carefully tear off the flap at the top, and when you open the triangle out, you'll have a square.

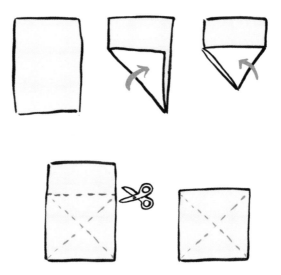

3. Now fold each of the four corners of the square into the middle of the square, making your fortune teller much smaller.

4. Turn the fortune teller over and place on a flat surface so that the folded triangles are face down. Now repeat the above step, folding the four corners facing you into the centre to make an even smaller square.

5. Lift up each of the triangles facing you and on each small triangle inside, write a wellbeing strategy or positive message. You should have eight triangles on which you can write eight messages.

6. On the four corners facing you, write the numbers from one to eight on the triangles.

7. Now flip the fortune teller over and on the four squares facing you, label each with a different colour, shape or item of your choice.

8. Flip it over again and place your forefingers and thumbs inside the pockets. Press into the centre and shape your fortune teller so that it is a bit like a flower.

9. Now your kids can play with it by asking another person to choose a colour, then a number, and finally revealing the message underneath.

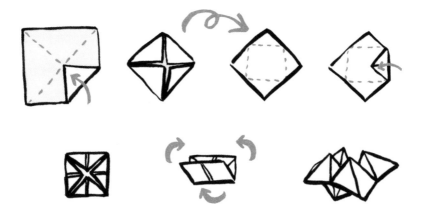

Wellbeing strategies – here are some ideas, however you can choose your own

• Take a photo of something that makes you happy

• Put on some music and do your favourite dance

• Draw a picture of something that makes you smile

• Put on your favourite piece of clothing

• Call or video chat with family or friends

• Read or have storytime with your favourite book

• Make a paper aeroplane and see how far it goes

• See how many hops you can do in one minute

TIMETABLE

Knowing how to fill time during the school holidays, or even over a long weekend, can be hard work with kids about. One way I've found to deal with this is having a simple timetable to give me a nudge and some much needed inspiration. I don't put any timings on it as it is really there to act as a list, but by spreading activities out over a few days, or a week, I can see the shape of what we might do and make sure we have a nice variety in store.

	MONDAY	TUESDAY	WEDNESDAY
ACHIEVABLE ART	Bubbles on Paper (42)		
TRIED & TESTED CRAFTS		Pom-Pom Wall Hanging (64)	
WHIZZY EASY SCIENCE			Bouncy Ball Eggs (80)
LET'S GET PHYSICAL			
SCREEN-FREE GAME TIME	Toothpick Towers (136)		
THE GREAT OUTDOORS		Bottle Bee Hotel (158)	
THE GREAT INDOORS			Let's Go Camping (177)
WELLBEING WONDERS		Origami Fortune Teller (214)	

I like to involve my girls and ask them what they'd like to do so that they feel in control and it also helps me to know what sort of mood they are in. I tend to aim for only a few activities a day and it really doesn't matter whether we do them or not. I usually feel better having a plan, even if we don't stick to it, and I've found that they are more likely to be up for doing an activity if they have thought about it beforehand.

THURSDAY	FRIDAY	SATURDAY	SUNDAY
		Magazine Collage (34)	
Magical Glow Jar (58)			
	Bread in a Bag (95)		
Home-made Sports Day (107)			Secret Agent Laser Challenge (102)
		Blindfold Sensory Challenge (129)	
	Butterfly Wings Three Ways (162)		
			Stargazing Extravaganza (188)
	Gratitude Tree (208)		

FINAL THOUGHT

I really hope that this book has given you lots of exciting new ways to spend time with your family and make the most of those moments in life when we don't know what to do next. When I started to write this book, I thought that it would, at best, be a handy resource for tired parents to reach for on a rainy weekend and I remain hopeful that this is the case! However, what I have also realised is that time with our kids is so precious, and that trying to make the most of it really is one of the best things we could do. Looking after kids in any capacity is no mean feat, however watching a child discover something new or listening to them belly laugh is a reminder of how special it is to spend time with small people. I hope that this book has equipped you to do just that, and that it will continue to be a little source of inspiration in the future.

'ENJOY THE LITTLE THINGS, FOR ONE DAY YOU MAY LOOK BACK AND REALISE THEY WERE THE BIG THINGS.'
Robert Brault, author

For more ideas, activities and inspiration or to share your own creations you can find me online **@TheWhatNowMum** or in the **Family Lockdown Tips & Ideas** Facebook group. I'd love to hear from you and see how you've made these ideas your own.

www.thewhatnowmum.com

Facebook: **www.facebook.com/thewhatnowmum**

Instagram: **@thewhatnowmum**

Twitter: **@TheWhatNowMum**

Facebook Group: **Family Lockdown Tips & Ideas**

ACKNOWLEDGMENTS

Firstly, I would like to thank the fantastic online 'Family Lockdown' community for their constant inspiration, energy and support. Without the group, there would be no book and I am so grateful to have been given the opportunity to share, in print, ideas inspired by them. The millions of posts, likes and comments in the group has turned our little corner of the internet into one of positivity and hope and remains to be my favourite virtual place to be.

Huge thanks go to the incredible team at Bluebird for being so encouraging and enthusiastic about the book, and for working at an astonishing speed to turn my dream into a reality. To Carole Tonkinson, Hockley Raven Spare, Jodie Mullish and the team, for everything. Thank you also to my wonderful agent Sophie Lambert for your expert guidance and for being so much fun to work with in bringing this all to fruition. And thank you to Mel Four for the truly wonderful illustrations in this book that have brought the activities to life.

To the team of admins and moderators who have helped me run the Facebook group, a heartfelt thank you. It would have been an impossible task without your enthusiasm, dedication, humour and virtual elbow grease. I can't begin to tell you how grateful I am for the countless hours you have volunteered to make the group the best it can possibly be, and for having such a laugh along the way.

To my mother, Hilary Simmons, for your constant love and kindness, and for being the best role model any daughter could have, thank you. You have kept me grounded during one of the most extraordinary times in my life and I hope you know that wanting to make the most of time with my own little family is rooted in the wonderful childhood I had with my sister Carina Simmons. I am constantly learning how to be a better parent from you and I hope, one day, to be the friend to Maisie and Georgie that you are to me. And to my late father, Derek Simmons, for imbuing in me the self-belief and 'can do' attitude that I know has made all of this possible.

To my husband Russell, for putting up with me constantly being on my phone, for turning a blind eye to yet another packet of biscuits mysteriously disappearing, for cheering me on when I didn't think I had it in me and for the endless cups of tea to keep me going. Thank you. You are my rock, and every day you make me happier. There is no-one I would rather spend my days with than you.

And finally, to my girls, Maisie and Georgie. My bold, courageous, brave and funny little girls, who keep me busier, happier and more fulfilled than I could ever have imagined. I'm sorry I have been a bit distracted, and that I've said 'just one more minute' a few too many times to get this book written. But I hope you'll see it was worth it. I love our time together more than anything in the world and I can't wait to see the people you will become. This book is ultimately for you, to show you what is possible, remind you what we did, and plan how we can spend our time together in the future.